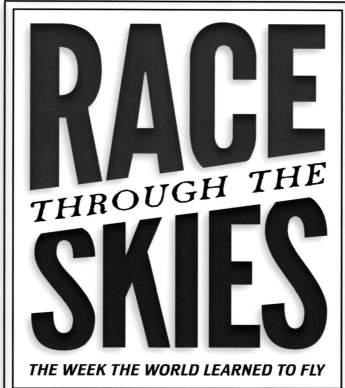

RACE
THROUGH THE
SKIES

THE WEEK THE WORLD LEARNED TO FLY

MARTIN W. SANDLER

BLOOMSBURY
CHILDREN'S BOOKS
NEW YORK LONDON OXFORD NEW DELHI SYDNEY

For Debby Perry,

with thanks and love

BLOOMSBURY CHILDREN'S BOOKS
Bloomsbury Publishing Inc., part of Bloomsbury Publishing Plc
1385 Broadway, New York, NY 10018

BLOOMSBURY, BLOOMSBURY CHILDREN'S BOOKS, and the Diana logo
are trademarks of Bloomsbury Publishing Plc

First published in the United States of America in July 2020
by Bloomsbury Children's Books

Text copyright © 2020 by Martin W. Sandler

All rights reserved. No part of this publication may be reproduced or transmitted
in any form or by any means, electronic or mechanical, including photocopying, recording,
or any information storage or retrieval system, without prior permission in writing from the publisher.

Bloomsbury Publishing Plc does not have any control over, or responsibility for, any third-party websites
referred to or in this book. All internet addresses given in this book were correct at the time of going to press.
The author and publisher regret any inconvenience caused if addresses have changed or sites have ceased to exist,
but can accept no responsibility for any such changes.

Bloomsbury books may be purchased for business or promotional use. For information on bulk purchases please contact
Macmillan Corporate and Premium Sales Department at specialmarkets@macmillan.com

Library of Congress Cataloging-in-Publication Data
Names: Sandler, Martin W., author.
Title: Race through the skies : the week the world learned to fly / by Martin W. Sandler.
Description: New York : Bloomsbury Children's Books, 2020. | Includes bibliographical references.
Identifiers: LCCN 2019046005
ISBN 978-1-5476-0344-2 (hardcover)
Subjects: LCSH: Aeronautics—History—Juvenile literature. | Airplanes—History—Juvenile literature. |
Wright, Orville, 1871–1948—Juvenile literature. | Wright, Wilbur, 1867–1912—Juvenile literature.
Classification: LCC TL547.S3233 2020 | DDC 629.1309—dc23
LC record available at https://lccn.loc.gov/2019046005

Book design by Patrick and Diane M. Collins
Printed in China by Leo Paper Products, Heshan, Guangdong
2 4 6 8 10 9 7 5 3 1

All papers used by Bloomsbury Publishing Plc are natural, recyclable products made from wood grown in
well-managed forests. The manufacturing processes conform to the environmental regulations of the country of origin.

To find out more about our authors and books visit www.bloomsbury.com and sign up for our newsletters.

CONTENTS

INTRODUCTION

IN THIS TIME when almost three million people fly on commercial airplanes every day within the United States alone and more than 43,000 flights take place daily, it is difficult to imagine that, little more than one hundred years ago, the airplane did not exist, and very few Americans had ever traveled more than twenty-five miles from where they were born. Equally difficult to envision is that there was a time when flight was the greatest of adventures.

That is what this book is all about. It is the story of how the notion of flight went from what was almost universally regarded as nothing more than an unrealistic dream to the most amazing achievement of the twentieth century and how one remarkable weeklong event was instrumental in the extraordinary development of this revolutionary mode of transportation. Above all else, here is an intensely human story, filled with some of history's most colorful and remarkable characters, people willing to risk all to fly higher, faster, and farther than anyone before them, always aware that, in their fragile airplanes, death was no more than a gust of wind or a broken wing strut away.

As this book reveals, the constant awareness of danger did nothing to dispel the lure of taking to the air felt by those who made flight a reality. Indeed, for many, it was one of the most compelling reasons for going aloft. Aside from the desire to win the cash prizes, gain the glory, and set the records, there were other reasons. And one of the world's first airplane passengers, Italian poet and novelist Gabriele D'Annunzio, spoke for untold numbers of others who followed when he exclaimed, "Until now I have never really lived! . . . It's in the air that one feels the glory of being [alive] and of conquering the elements. There is the exquisite smoothness of motion and the joy of gliding through space. It is powerful. Can I not express it in poetry? I might try."

It is also the intention of this book to dispel many myths that have surrounded the birth of flight—for instance, it was not at Kitty Hawk, North Carolina, in 1903, but in France in 1909, that Wilbur Wright proved that he and his brother had actually flown and that he showed many of the first spectators ever to publicly view a plane in flight, including many future giants of the air, how it was done.

Spectators at the Rheims air meet get a close-up look at an "airoplane." For many it was their first view of the machine that would change the world.

At the heart of this book is a fascinating saga unto itself, the story of the most important week in aviation history, the Great Aviation Week at Rheims, during which the idea of the airplane became a practical fact and the age of aviation truly began.

That it began, and that it has affected our lives in so many ways, is unquestionably one of the most important stories in all of human history, a story filled with more than its share of improbabilities and magic. For as pioneer aviation legend Igor Sikorsky declared and as this book reveals, "Aeronautics was neither an industry nor even a science. . . . It was a miracle."

AVIATION BEFORE RHEIMS

ON THE EVENING of December 17, 1903, Lorin Wright, the brother of two Dayton, Ohio, bicycle makers, took a news release he had prepared to the offices of the *Dayton Daily Journal.* There he handed it to the newspaper's telegraph editor, the man in charge of wiring news stories of interest to papers throughout America and much of the world. The news release reported that earlier that day the brothers, named Wilbur and Orville, had achieved what had been one of humankind's oldest and greatest dreams. They had flown in a heavier-than-air powered flying machine for fifty-seven seconds.

The editor's response was not what Lorin expected. "Fifty-seven

Wilbur Wright runs along as his brother Orville pilots the first powered flight. The photograph was taken by John T. Daniels, a member of the U.S. Life-Saving Station at Kill Devil Hills, North Carolina.

Orville Wright piloting the Flyer III above Huffman Prairie, Ohio. Also known as Huffman Prairie Flying Field, it would later become a hub for innovation in early American aviation.

seconds, hey?" the newspaperman said. "If it had been fifty-seven min-utes, then it might have been a news item." Actually, the telegraph editor didn't really believe that the Wrights had flown at all. The famous scientist Samuel Langley, who was also the head of the Smithsonian Institution, had failed spectacularly in a flight attempt only nine days earlier, so how could two unknown Dayton residents have succeeded?

Although he was holding in his hands one of the greatest news scoops of all time, the editor ignored it. Instead, the main story on the front page of the next day's *Journal* was all about the excellent Christmas business that the local stores were enjoying. Other stories reported on the weekly meeting of a trade union, the pardoning of a robber, and the arrest of a pickpocket. Nowhere in the entire paper was there a single word about what had taken place in Kitty Hawk, North Carolina, the previous day.

Wilbur and Orville Wright weren't that disappointed, though. They knew that their airplane needed a great many improvements if it was to become a practical means of transportation. Just as important to them, they were determined not to demonstrate their plane publicly until they perfected it. They were also determined to discourage all competitors by obtaining patents on the various parts of their flying machine.

In 1904, the Wright brothers set up a shop at Huffman Prairie, an eighty-four-acre pasture some eight miles east of Dayton. There they worked night and day to build a more advanced and practical version of their airplane. Before the year was out, they had built the Flyer II, in which they executed the first complete turn ever made by a flying machine. They had also constructed the craft in such a way that, rather than lying prone on the fuselage, the pilot (and passenger if desired) could ride in a sitting position.

The Wrights kept making improvements, and in June 1905, the Flyer III, the world's first truly practical airplane, took to the air. On October 5, 1905, it flew for an astounding 39.5 minutes and covered over 24 miles. It was the first airplane that could bank, circle, and fly figure eights. Eventually, it would be able to stay up in the air

IT WAS THE FIRST AIRPLANE THAT COULD BANK, CIRCLE, AND FLY FIGURE EIGHTS

for an hour at a time. It incorporated what was perhaps the Wrights' greatest innovation, a system called "warping," by which the tips of the airplane's wings could be maneuvered to allow for graceful turns and unprecedented agility.

The brothers then stopped flying completely. Instead, they devoted all their time to securing their patents and selling their airplanes. Amazingly, it would take almost three more years before the world would begin to learn what these two self-educated, unassuming men from Ohio had done.

Orville Wright's demonstrations for the U.S. Army at Fort Myer, Virginia, were the brothers' first public flights. Spectators were thrilled as they saw an airplane aloft for the first time.

During those three years, people on both sides of the Atlantic had grown increasingly skeptical as to whether or not the Wrights had actually flown. "The Wrights have flown or they have not flown," exclaimed the *New York Herald* in 1906. "They are . . . either fliers or liars. It is difficult to fly. It is easy to say, 'We have flown.'"

By 1908, however, things were about to change. By this time, the brothers had secured their patents and had gotten their initial contracts to manufacture aircraft. They were ready to stage their first public flights, anxious to show the world that not only had they indeed flown, but they had also developed an airplane far more advanced than anyone could imagine.

For the first time in their long years working together, the brothers decided to split up. Hoping to get contracts to build aircraft for the United States Army, Orville arranged for a series of demonstration flights for military and government officials at Fort Myer, Virginia. Wilbur was to travel to Europe to show off his flying skills to the highly dubious population there, particularly the French, who, thanks to a number of bold pioneer aviators, were claiming supremacy in the sky.

⤳ THE WRIGHTS IN EUROPE ⤳

WILBUR ARRIVED IN FRANCE on May 29 1908, aware that Orville had packed and then shipped the disassembled latest Wright Flyer in crates to the port of Le Havre. But when Wilbur opened the crates he got one of the greatest shocks of his life. Rather than being arranged in a way that would make their assembly as easy a task as possible, the various parts of the plane seemed to have been tossed into the boxes in a totally haphazard manner. To make matters worse, the aircraft's cloth covering was badly ripped and the plane's axles had been bent. A dismayed Wilbur sent off a letter to his brother. "I opened the boxes yesterday," he wrote, "and have been puzzled ever since to know how you could have wasted two whole days packing them."

In reality, Orville had packed the parts of the Flyer as carefully and as properly as could be done. The fault lay with the French customs officials who, after removing the parts from the crates for inspection, had clumsily thrown them back into the boxes before resealing them. Relieved as he was to find out that it was not his brother's fault, it still left Wilbur with an enormous problem: Where and how was he going to be able to get the Flyer back in shape to make his flights?

Fortunately, despite all the detractors the Wrights had in France, there was one man who believed they had flown, an admirer named Léon Bollée. An automobile manufacturer and a sport balloonist, Bollée had a factory near the racetrack at Le Mans. Graciously, he offered

Wilbur both the use of the factory to reassemble his plane and the aid of the mechanics who worked there.

By mid-June 1908, Wilbur was hard at work. As word of his presence and what he was doing spread, he was contacted by several notable individuals, including Charles Stewart Rolls, founder of the Rolls-Royce automobile company, and Henry Farman, a French pilot who was making headlines with some of his flying feats. Wilbur would never forget how another of the young French aviators, who was also showing great promise, had before Bollée came to the rescue, offered Wilbur the use of his shop. His name was Louis Blériot.

For the majority of the French population, until Wilbur Wright showed that he could really fly, the jury was still out about the American. But that was not true of those who worked with the Wright brother at Bollée's factory. They marveled at his craftsmanship and how, when needed, he made his own parts for his plane. But mostly they were astounded by how long and how hard he worked. And, for a person they regarded as a "famous American," they could not get over how simply he lived while the plane was being assembled. A reporter for the *Daily Mail* shared their view, writing:

> *In a corner of the shed was his "room." This consisted of a low packing case from which the top had been removed. Resting on the edges of the case was a narrow truckle bed. Nailed to the sides of the shed was a piece of looking glass and close by a camp washstand. This together with a cabin trunk, a small petrol cooking stove—he cooks his own breakfast—and a camp stool, comprised the whole furniture. He takes his baths from a hosepipe attached to a*

well sixty feet away. He sleeps practically under the wings of his aeroplane. And early in the day he starts to work, whistling the while.

Finally, in the first week of August 1908, Wilbur suddenly exclaimed that he felt that "it would be a good thing to do a little something." It was time to prove what he and the Flyer could do. Saturday, August 8, 1908, the day chosen for the long-anticipated flight, turned out to be ideal for flying—sunny, with just a light wind. Word that Wilbur was at last going to take to the air spread rapidly, and a large crowd began filling up the wooden grandstands at the racetrack outside Le Mans, where the flight would take place. Scattered through the crowd were

Wilbur Wright during one of his early flight demonstrations at Hunaudières racecourse near Le Mans, France. He would astound everyone in attendance with his skill and daring.

reporters and correspondents from London, Paris, New York, and other major cities around the world, all wondering if they were about to cover one of the most important stories of their time. It was the largest and most knowledgeable gathering that had ever witnessed a Wright flight, including officials from various French embassies, noted aviation writer François Peyrey, and Louis Blériot, Hubert Latham, and other French airmen.

Also among the throng were those who could hardly be regarded as Wright enthusiasts. Certain that the Wrights had never flown and believing that the title "first to fly" belonged to either Brazilian Alberto Santos-Dumont, who had achieved a brief flight in 1906, or to Henry Farman, who had flown a three-fifths-of-a-mile circuit earlier in 1908, many of these doubters had come to Le Mans both hoping and expecting that Wilbur would fail.

MANY OF THESE DOUBTERS HAD COME TO LE MANS BOTH HOPING AND EXPECTING THAT WILBUR WOULD FAIL.

Most vocal among them was French Aero Club official Ernest Archdeacon. At an Aero Club dinner in October 1907, he had stated, "The famous Wright Brothers may today claim all they wish. If it is true—and I doubt it more and more—that they were the first to fly through the air, they will not have the glory before History. They would only have had to eschew these incomprehensible affectations of mystery and to carry out their experiments in broad daylight, like Santos-Dumont and Farman, and before official judges, surrounded by thousands of spectators." Now, on a small racetrack near Le Mans, France, that was exactly what was about to happen.

It was midafternoon when Wilbur and the mechanics rolled the sparkling-white Flyer out of its shed. According to one of Wright's associates, Hart Berg, in spite of the huge importance of the occasion, Wilbur was his usual quiet, confident self. "One thing," recalled Berg, "that, to me at least, made his appearance all the more dramatic, was that he was not dressed as if about to do something daring or unusual. He, of course, had no special pilot's helmet or jacket, since no such garb yet existed, but appeared in the ordinary gray suit he usually wore, and a cap. And he had on, as he nearly always did when not in overalls, a high starched collar."

For what seemed like an inordinately long time, Wilbur walked around and around his plane, checking and rechecking every detail. Then he walked back and forth along the path the Flyer would travel in taking off. Finally, he turned his cap backward and then stated simply to those standing next to the plane, "Gentlemen, I'm going to fly."

While the crowd seemed to hold its breath, the aircraft's engine started with a roar—and then quickly died. A collar stud on the back of Wilbur's shirt had caught on one of the plane's wires. When it was freed, the engine came to life again, and Wilbur's flight was underway. As the Flyer made its ascent, even those spectators who had not seen a flight before knew they were witnessing something very special.

Most of those in the crowd had expected that, at best, Wilbur would fly for a short distance in a straight line. Instead, after completing four graceful, steeply banked turns, he stunned the onlookers by performing two full figure eights. Then he made three long, smooth circuits around the racetrack before landing easily about 50 feet from the spot from which he had taken off. He had been in the air for less than 2 minutes and had flown 2 miles.

The spectators could hardly believe what they had seen. Before Wilbur even landed, they were cheering wildly, throwing hats into the air. As soon as Wilbur stepped down from the plane he was mobbed. "We are as children compared with the Wrights," commented one onlooker.

"A new era in . . . flight has commenced," stated another. All agreed with the shouts that rang out, exclaiming, "This man has conquered the air. He is not a bluffer."

The next day the press was beside itself with the praise for what had taken place at Le Mans. "It was not merely a success," stated *Le Figaro*. "[It] was a decisive victory for aviation, the news of which will revolutionize scientific circles through the world." *The Daily Mail* proclaimed it was "the most marvelous aeroplane flight *ever* witnessed on this side of the Atlantic."

Perhaps the simplest and yet most impressive reaction came from two small boys who had snuck in under a fence to watch the spectacle. Climbing aboard their bicycles, they pedaled furiously toward Le Mans to spread the news, shouting, "*Il vole, il vole*—he flies, he flies."

There was no question—Wilbur Wright had taken France by storm. And over the next five months the acclaim grew even greater as he staged flight after flight and stayed aloft longer and longer. Eventually, the crowds attending these events would grow so large that tickets of admission would have to be sold. On August 10, more than two thousand people came to watch Wilbur's flight. Three days later, before the largest crowd yet, he completed the longest flight at Le Mans thus far. Every flight was filled with its own special thrills for the ever-growing crowds. "In a flight lasting 32 seconds," the *Daily Mail* reported, "[Wilbur] took a complete turn within a radius of thirty yards and alighted with the ease of a bird in the midst of the field." It was, exclaimed the newspaper, "The most magnificent turning movement that has *ever* been performed by an aviator." The same evening Wilbur, in yet another flight, made two huge figure eights, the largest that had *ever* been seen in Europe. Even when things went badly, the amazing pilot seemed to come out on top. On one of the flights his left wing hit the ground, resulting in what Wright admitted was a "pretty bad smash-up." Yet the crowd could not

help but be impressed with the way he handled the Flyer throughout the mishap. Quoting a French aircraft designer who witnessed the incident, the *New York Herald* declared that "Mr. Wright is as superb in his accidents as he is in his flights."

With each flight, Wilbur's popularity rose. Postcards depicting him and his plane sold by the thousands. A new song titled "Il Vole" became a huge hit.

To Wilbur, it was simply overwhelming. "All the children within a dozen miles of my camp know me," he wrote to his brother, "and as I ride along the roads they politely take off their hats and smile and say, 'Bonjour Monsieur Wright.' They are really almost the only ones,

On October 7, 1908, at Camp d'Auvours, France, Mrs. Edith Berg became Wilbur Wright's first woman passenger when they flew for two minutes. Mrs. Berg tied her skirt below her knees for decorum.

except close friends, who know how to pronounce my name." To his sister he wrote, "I cannot even take a bath without having a hundred or two people peeking at me." And in a letter to his father he told him, "Every evening a crowd of two or three thousand people comes out to see if I will make a flight, and goes home disappointed if I do not. Some of them have come twenty, forty, or even sixty miles on bicycles. . . . Once an old man of seventy living about thirty miles away, made the round trip on a bicycle every day for nearly a week."

Wilbur flew at Le Mans for six months. During that time more than 200,000 people came to watch him. To the crowd's delight, he had begun taking passengers up with him. On October 6, he made the first flight with a passenger that had *ever* lasted more than an hour. By October 15 he had taken a total of thirty people aloft. That was more passengers than all the European aviators put together. One who accompanied Wilbur was the reporter for the French magazine *Le Figaro.* "I have known today a magnificent intoxication," he wrote after landing. "I have learnt how it feels to be a bird. I have flown. Yes, I have flown. I am still astounded at it, still deeply moved."

Also among those who joined Wilbur was Léon Bollée, the man who had generously lent the aviator his factory for the assembly of the Flyer. In these early days of flight, strict limits were put on how much a passenger could weigh. Bollée weighed 240 pounds! "I took Bollee for a couple of rounds of the field this morning . . . ," Wilbur wrote home. "It created more astonishment than anything else I have done."

Along with his other motives, one of the reasons that Wilbur had decided to make his European demonstrations was to show that, when operated by an experienced pilot, flying machines could be safe as well as spectacular. Thus, it was not surprising that, along with giving rides to passengers, he also began giving flying lessons. The first person in France he taught was Charles, the Comte de Lambert, who would later become one of the best known of the early French aviators and one of early flight's most articulate spokespersons.

Before 1908 was over, Wilbur Wright had done much more than quiet those who had doubted that he and his brother had ever flown. As he continued to make flight after flight, his aerial demonstrations lasted longer and longer until he shattered two of the most important early flight records. On December 18, he set a new altitude record at 375 feet. Then, on the final day of the year, he once again astounded the aviation world. He had already set the distance/duration record several times, but on December 31, 1908, flying through freezing mist, he established an amazing new mark by flying 77.48 miles in just over 2 hours and 20 minutes.

"I HAVE KNOWN TODAY A MAGNIFICENT INTOXICATION. I HAVE LEARNT HOW IT FEELS TO BE A BIRD. I HAVE FLOWN."

"The year finishes with a new burst of thunder," wrote French journalist Georges Prade. "One more time, the eagle has taken flight and has astonished by the power of his wings. It really seems like this mysterious man likes to surprise us. . . . With this flight of 75 miles, his sudden climbs to more than 300 feet up in the clouds . . . he remains the man of the year, and I apologize for having found such a miserable epithet to characterize the man who will very likely be the man of the century."

The year had ended on a high note indeed, and on January 16, 1909, things got even better. Orville and the Wrights' sister, Katharine, joined Wilbur in Europe.

Orville had spent the better part of four months demonstrating the Flyer for army and government officials. He had given his first demonstrations on September 9, 1908, when, early in the morning, he circled the field at Fort Myer fifty-seven times in fifty-seven minutes

and twenty-five seconds. In the next three weeks he broke his personal records for distance and endurance and for the length of time carrying a passenger with him. But it had not been all glory. Even though the Flyer was formally purchased by the United States government, there had been a devastating incident. On September 17, 1908, Orville and one of the army officials, Lieutenant Thomas E. Selfridge, were aloft in the Flyer when one of the aircraft's propellers suddenly snapped and clipped off a wire that held the tail in place, sending the plane into a deadly dive. Rescuers pulled a bleeding and unconscious Orville from the wreckage. He had suffered a broken leg, broken ribs, and an injured back. But he would live. Lieutenant Selfridge was not as fortunate. He passed away on an operating table, the first person ever to die from an accident while riding in a heavier-than-air powered aircraft.

Orville and Katharine arrived in Le Mans just as the weather in that part of France was turning cold. Soon they and Wilbur, seeking a warmer climate, moved to the city of Pau in the southern part of the country, where the adulation for Wilbur (and for Orville, now that it had been proven that the brothers had indeed flown at Kitty Hawk) reached almost fever pitch. Kings, queens, and members of high society made pilgrimages to Pau to witness Wilbur in flight and have themselves photographed with the brothers. Reporters, authors, people with business deals, and other aviators sought their attention. There was no escaping the adulation. When Wilbur sought some peace and relaxation by taking a sightseeing trip to the French Senate, the legislators abruptly halted their deliberations and gave him a standing ovation.

The three Wrights spent the better part of April 1909 in Italy, where Wilbur had trained two pilots for the Italian army. But once it became apparent that much of their adoring public had followed them to Italy ("Princes and millionaires are as thick as thieves," exclaimed Wilbur), they felt it was time to return home.

Facing page: Spectators work feverishly to free Orville Wright from the wreckage of his plane following his crash at Fort Myer, Virginia, on September 17, 1908. Those in the group at the right in the photograph were worrying about Wright's passenger, Lieutenant Thomas Selfridge.

The time in Europe had been extraordinary for Wilbur in particular. He had given the world its first lessons in flight. And, as his very first pupil, Comte de Lambert, would explain, he had done much more. "There are no limits to this enterprise of navigating the air except the limits of the atmosphere itself," Lambert wrote after completing his lessons with Wright. "Wherever the air is, man can go—that has been demonstrated. [We are living in] the epochal years of the history of man on earth—or, rather, the end of the epoch of man on earth and the beginning of the era of man above the earth."

~ FLYING THE CHANNEL ~

ONE OF THE TENS OF THOUSANDS who had witnessed at least one of Wilbur Wright's flying demonstrations was an Englishman named Alfred Harmsworth. Better known as Lord Northcliffe, he was the owner of the British newspaper the London *Daily Mail.* In October 1908, Northcliffe, destined to become one of aviation's earliest and greatest champions, had offered a prize of one thousand English pounds to whoever could fly across the English Channel from coast to coast in either direction.

FAR MORE COMMON WAS THE DENSE FOG THAT COULD PLUNGE AN AVIATOR INTO COMPLETE DARKNESS. BUT MOST OF ALL THERE WAS THE WIND, THE GREATEST ENEMY.

Northcliffe was not the first to have thought of the idea of offering prize money to motivate aviators. The practice began with Ernest Archdeacon and oil industrialist Henri Deutsch de la Meurthe. In 1903, in what was the first prize to encourage powered flight, they offered 50,000 francs to the first pilot to fly a heavier-than-air machine for a distance of 25 meters (82 feet).

According to the rules of the contest that Lord Northcliffe sponsored in 1908, the flight across the English Channel had to be made between sunrise and sunset. The offer was enticing, a chance for both glory and a great deal of money.

It presented an enormous challenge as well. One that few, no matter how brave, were inclined to take. At its narrowest point, the Channel stretched some twenty miles from the cliffs of Dover in England to the bleak headlands near Calais on the coast of France. Even more daunting was the weather that would have to be overcome. Fair weather was extremely rare. Far more common was the dense fog that could plunge an aviator into complete darkness. So too was the constant rain, a particular foe of the early "birdmen" in their open cockpits. But most of all there was the wind, the greatest enemy. Over the Channel, air swirls in every direction and constant winds result, slamming into hills on both the English and French coasts, gusting into unique, powerful currents that could tear apart an early aircraft.

Still, given the excitement for flying that Wilbur Wright had stirred, Lord Northcliffe was certain that there would be several daring souls willing to take the chance, especially Wright himself. But to Northcliffe's and many others' surprise, Wright made it clear that he preferred to spend his time back in the United States working to make the Wright Company as big a success as possible. In the end, only two aviators attempted the flight: Hubert Latham, a French daredevil who had taken up flying because he feared he had tuberculosis and said he preferred a sudden death to a lingering one, and Louis Blériot, the French aviator who had been inspired by Wilbur Wright's flying exhibitions—and who was known among his fellow aviators as *l'homme qui tombe toujours* (the man who always crashes).

In early July 1909, Latham, his mechanics, and other helpers had set up camp in the small French village of Sangatte, a few miles from

Calais. With Latham was one of the world's earliest airplane designers, Léon Levavasseur, the man who had built the monoplane that Latham would be flying.

The fact that Latham's attempt was delayed for several days by heavy winds and driving rain only added to the excitement and the tension. Every morning, hordes of spectators arrived at the camp hoping to see the launch of such a historic event. Across the Channel in Dover, England, thousands of onlookers arrived by train, hoping to be present in case the aviator actually made it across. Harbors on both sides of the Channel filled up with boats carrying legions of other expectant onlookers. In England, the White Star Line delayed the departure of one of its United States–bound luxury cruise ships so that its passengers could watch the attempted flights.

Finally, on July 19, 1909, the weather cleared and Latham took off on his quest for glory. For the first 7.5 miles of his flight it appeared that he was well on his way to the coveted prize. But then, just as he was about to take a picture of the destroyer *Harpon* that the French government had assigned to him to act as a rescue vessel if needed, his engine began to cough. Then it sputtered. Then it stopped completely.

Members of the French navy work to recover Hubert Latham's airplane from the sea. Like other setbacks in his life, the crash did not deter him from striving to become the first to fly across the English Channel.

Latham's plane glided into the water, with the wings and tail keeping the plane afloat until the destroyer arrived minutes later. When the launch from the *Harpon* reached him, the aviator was leaning back in his seat calmly smoking a cigarette, which only added to the growing legend around him. And there was something else that would add to the mystique: Hubert Latham had become the first pilot in history to crash an airplane into the sea . . . and he survived.

Taken back to Calais wearing a French naval officer's raincoat and a sailor's hat with a pom-pom on it, he first kissed a young woman onlooker and then announced that after taking a steam bath he would begin preparing for a second try with a new aircraft. "I wasn't lucky this time," Latham declared, "but the Channel will be conquered. I'm starting over and I will succeed."

Latham's well-publicized ditch into the sea inspired Blériot to make a spur-of-the-moment decision to go after Lord Northcliffe's *Daily Mail* prize. Born in the north of France, Blériot had studied engineering at the prestigious L'École Centrale des Arts et Manufactures. He had gone on to earn a fortune by inventing and then manufacturing the first headlamps for automobiles. Between 1901 and 1909, however, his wealth diminished rapidly as he fell in love with flying and built and crashed a series of airplanes, most of which were not airworthy. Then, in the spring of 1909, he managed to design and build a plane he named Blériot XI that was far better than anything he had ever created. By this time, however, he was almost completely out of money, so much so that he lacked the funds to mount an attempt to cross the Channel. It was here that Blériot's wife, Alicia, the mother of his six children, saved the day, and in a most unusual fashion.

In July 1909, Alicia Blériot was in Paris visiting the family of an extremely rich Haitian plantation owner when the man's young son climbed onto the balcony of the apartment. Losing his balance, he was about to fall off when Mrs. Blériot grabbed him, probably saving his life. The grateful Haitian planter, hearing what Alicia Blériot's husband wanted to do, agreed to finance Blériot's Channel-crossing attempt. For the flier, it was a lifesaving development. "I had to keep going," he later wrote, "because, like a gambler, I had to recoup my losses. I had to fly."

UNLIKE THE ANTOINETTE, THE BLÉRIOT XI HAD NO NAVIGATIONAL INSTRUMENTS OF ANY KIND, NOT EVEN A COMPASS.

Determined to launch his flight before Latham could make a second attempt, Blériot and his entourage of mechanics, advisers, engineers, and journalists set up camp at Les Baraques, a few miles from Calais. But, as had happened with Latham, Mother Nature was against him. Day after day, gale-force winds and pounding rain made it impossible for Blériot to take off.

It was not his only problem. During a recent endurance competition, a part of his plane's exhaust pipe had come loose and Blériot's foot had been so severely burned that he could walk only with the aid of crutches. Still, after Latham and his crew returned to their camp at Sangatte and began feverishly assembling a new plane, Blériot declared that his injured foot would not stop him from taking off as soon as he could. "In exploits of this sort," he declared, "whatever they are worth, it's only the first that counts."

Truth be told, it was not only the horrendous weather and his injured foot that put Blériot at a disadvantage in his contest with Latham. The Blériot XI was a far inferior plane to Latham's graceful, larger Antoinette. And, unlike the Antoinette, the Blériot XI had no navigational instruments of any kind, not even a compass.

On the other hand, Blériot had an important thing going for him.

His chances of making it across the Channel depended on the reliability of his engine, and his had been made by an Italian named Alessandro Anzani, who, when he was not racing bicycles, made motorcycle engines. His engines were the furthest thing from fancy or polished, but they had an enormous redeeming virtue. They kept on running. More than anything else, it was his faith in his engine that gave Blériot the confidence that he could make it across the Channel.

He had gained confidence in something else as well—solving the major challenge of finding a landing place on the unfamiliar English side of the Channel. Blériot knew the beachfront at Dover was too narrow to accommodate a landing and that the famous Shakespeare Cliff there was too high for him to fly over, looking for a landing spot beyond. But a French reporter named Charles Fontaine had been sent by his paper to cover Blériot's arrival, should it take place. Anxious to help Blériot win the glory for France, Fontaine found a suitable landing place between the cliff and the beach and bought picture postcards of the spot. He then marked the landing site with an *X* on the postcards and sent these to Blériot via the Channel ferry, along with a note telling the pilot he would be standing on the spot waving a large French flag.

By this time, interest in what was going on in both the Latham and Blériot camps had reached a fever pitch. People had traveled from as far as Paris and London to witness what they hoped would be a historic event. An event that had turned into a genuine race. Who would be the first to take off, Latham or Blériot? Most important, would one of them make it safely across? What was clear was that answers to those questions would have to wait until the relentless wind and rain died down.

On the night of Saturday, July 24, Latham went to bed leaving strict orders with his mechanics that he should be awakened at 3:30 a.m. if the wind died down sufficiently to allow a takeoff. By 3:30 the wind had become much calmer, but for some reason, never fully explained,

The beginning of a historic flight. Louis Blériot stands in his airplane as he and his crew prepare the plane for the attempt to fly across the English Channel.

Latham's helpers let him sleep on. In the Blériot camp, however, things were much different. As soon as it had become obvious that the wind had diminished and the sky was clearing, a car was sent to bring the pilot back from his hotel. He had arisen grumpily, later admitting, "I would have been happy if they'd told me that the wind was blowing so hard there was no point in even trying."

But by the time Blériot got to his camp, took up a pair of binoculars, looked toward Sangatte and the Latham camp, and saw that nothing was stirring, his mood had changed dramatically. He could be in the air before Latham even knew he was on his way. At 4:35 a.m. he climbed into the Blériot XI and took it for a brief test run. Returning without incident, he was shouting to his mechanic even before he had come to a complete stop. "Replace the fuel," he bellowed. "In ten minutes I start for England."

According to the rules of the contest, the flight attempt had to be sometime between sunrise and sunset, and as anxious as he was to be off, Blériot had to wait until 4:41 a.m. before he was told that sunrise had officially begun. Four minutes later, dressed in a khaki jacket lined with wool for warmth, tweed shirt and trousers, and a tight-fitting cap fastened over his head and ears, the pilot signaled he was ready.

At 4:45 a.m., July 25, 1909, filled with no small amount of anxiety, he took off. For the spectators who, despite the early hour, had remained at Les Baraques hoping to see what could be a historic take-off, Blériot's departure elicited feelings common at a time when it was still difficult for many to believe that people could actually fly. Among them was the *Daily Mail* reporter Harry Harper. "Again," he wrote, "I felt that overpowering rush of excitement which I find almost everyone has experienced who has seen a man fly. It is an exhilaration, a thrill, an ecstasy. Just as children jump and clap their hands to see a kite mount, so, when the machine leaves the ground and with a soaring movement really flies upon its spreading wings, one feels impelled to shout, to rush after it, to do anything which will relieve the overcharged emotion."

Meantime, Latham's mechanics and advisers felt no such ecstasy. Realizing they had been outmaneuvered, they rushed to wake up their pilot, who quickly donned his flying clothes and ordered that his plane be made ready. But by this time the wind had once again begun to howl, making a takeoff much too dangerous to attempt.

Latham was despondent over his lost opportunity but he was not without hope. The fact that Blériot was over the Channel hardly guaranteed that he'd make it all the way. Far from it. With all his accomplishments, wasn't this the pilot perhaps best known for the amazing number of crashes—thirty-five!—he had experienced? And given the heavy winds that had come back up almost immediately after Blériot had taken off, wasn't there a good chance that he'd be blown off course and end up who knows where?

Truth be told, Blériot was already experiencing serious difficulty.

"IT IS AN EXHILARATION, A THRILL, AN ECSTASY."

"For ten minutes [after taking off]," he would later write, "I was alone, isolated, lost in the middle of the [clouds], seeing nothing on the horizon, not even a boat." But then just as suddenly as he had become lost in the clouds, they parted and below him he could see the French naval vessel that had been sent to guide him across the Channel. By the time he reached mid-Channel he had become absolutely euphoric, confident that he had nothing but clear sailing ahead. So confident that he raced ahead of the *Escopette*, abandoning his lifeline. It was a mistake. Once again huge banks of clouds swept in, engulfing him completely. Blériot was actually being swept northward past Dover, toward the North Sea. It would have been a fatal development, but again his

Both Blériot's and Latham's flights captured great attention. Here a group of well-wishers watches intently as Blériot heads out over the Channel.

Young people were among those who gathered on the shores of Calais to cheer on Blériot. His accomplishment would be one of the first great achievements in the history of manned, powered flight.

luck turned: the clouds parted and beneath him he could see three ships speeding along. He couldn't tell exactly what type of vessels they were, but they were obviously heading for a port. "Dover, no doubt," he later wrote, "so I calmly followed them. The sailors were cheering enthusiastically. I almost wanted to ask them the way to Dover. Alas, I didn't speak English." Soon, he found himself flying along a high and foreboding cliff. He had reached England. At this point the wind was blowing stronger than at any time since he had taken off. Then he spotted what might well have been the most welcome sight of his life. "Suddenly," he later recounted, "at the edge of an opening that appeared in the cliff, I saw a man desperately waving a [French] flag, out alone in the middle of a field, shouting 'Bravo! Bravo!'" Charles Fontaine had kept his promise.

Nosing himself and his plane straight down from a height of 65 feet, Blériot crashed rather than landed, not far from where Fontaine was wildly cheering. Leaving the plane, the aviator could not help but notice that one of its propellers was completely destroyed, as was its undercarriage. As aviation historian Robert Wohl has written, "Given his reputation as a pilot hard on airplanes, it was only appropriate that Blériot's epoch-making flight should end with a crash." As for Blériot, his response to his far-from-perfect landing was simple. "So what?" he stated. "I had crossed the Channel."

Once out of the plane Blériot was embraced by Fontaine, who, after kissing him enthusiastically on both cheeks, wrapped him in the French flag. It was 5:18 a.m. The 21-mile flight had taken just 37 minutes. In that short space of time Louis Blériot had not only flown into England, he had flown into history.

As for Latham, as soon as he received word that Blériot had landed in England, he adopted a new resolve. Deciding that if he could not be first, he could be a proud second, and he once again took off across the

Channel. But within sight of Dover, his engine quit on him again and for the second time he plunged into the sea. This time there would be no smooth landing, no stress-free waiting for a rescue. He came down hard, gashing his head seriously, and only a quick response from a ship in the area saved him from drowning. Both for his graciousness toward his rival and his determination to succeed, Latham would become more popular than ever. Blériot would join the ranks of the world's greatest celebrities, something with which he would never be comfortable.

The tributes had begun pouring in almost as soon as Blériot had landed, and the *Daily Mail* characterized the flight as "the dawn of a new age for [humanity]." The aviator accepted his prize from Lord

Louis Blériot poses with his wife and airplane after his English Channel flight. Blériot immediately became aviation's greatest hero.

Northcliffe at a giant celebration, and when he returned to France, more than 100,000 people were waiting to greet him.

The banquets, testimonials, and other forms of celebration continued for weeks. And with each passing day, it became increasingly apparent that Blériot's triumph, historically important as it was, signified something far more elemental than the first powered flight across the English Channel. "What," asked Gaston Calmette, the highly respected editor of the magazine *Le Figaro*, "will become of man's laws . . . the commercial exchanges, their defenses, their relations, their intercourse, on the day when man can, by the action of his will alone, pass in a few hours beyond all horizons, across all oceans, and above all rivers . . . ?" Calmette had a ready answer to his own question: "Within the foreseeable future," he concluded, "the conditions of human life will be profoundly changed."

Prior to that date, other pilots had flown much farther than the 21 miles that Blériot had traveled. Other aviators had stayed in the air much longer than the 37 minutes that he had spent over the English Channel. But his crossing over such a vital natural boundary between two countries had a very special meaning. By bringing two nations closer together physically than ever before, Blériot had shrunk both time and distance. As one historian put it, "It was as if that single flight had suddenly redrawn the map of the world."

RHEIMS:
THE
PREPARATIONS

LOUIS BLÉRIOT'S cross-Channel flight startled people everywhere. And with good reason. A few months before the historic event no airplane flight had ever taken place in all Great Britain. A few weeks before Blériot's achievement there were fewer than sixty airplanes in the entire world. Yet only one month after the Channel was crossed another happening became even more important in establishing the presence and practicality of heavier-than-air flight.

Named the Grande Semaine d'Aviation de la Champagne (the Champagne Region's Great Aviation Week) and held outside the ancient cathedral city of Rheims (also known as Reims) in France, it

The Rheims air meet, the first international event of its kind, was highly promoted. This was the official poster for the meeting.

was the first-ever international air meet. The event would be gigantic, one that would require serious sponsorship. And it received it.

Beginning in November 1908, the Rheims air meet was carefully organized by a committee of investors that called itself the Champagnie Generale de l'Aerolocomotion. It was headed by the Marquis de Polignac, the manager of one of the region's leading champagne-producing companies. The influential marquis, who was convinced that the Great Aviation Week would not only introduce aviation to the world but would be a giant profit-maker as well, was instrumental in persuading officials of the area's other leading champagne houses to join the committee and have their companies invest heavily in the meet.

The champagne houses were not the only ones to contribute to the Grande Semaine's success. The city of Rheims also invested heavily in the meet. And import-ant organizational assistance was received from the Automobile Club du France, which had experience in putting together automobile races, and from the French Areo Club, which agreed to over-see the week-long competition. England's future prime minis-ter David Lloyd George put the importance of the event simply. "Before Rheims," he declared,

Rheims cathedral.

EGLISE CATHEDRALE A REIMS
TRANSSEPT — CROISILLON SEPTENTRIONAL — ELEVATION EXTERIEURE

"the practicality of flight was in doubt. After Rheims, it was a demonstrated fact."

As some news correspondents pointed out, not since Joan of Arc had arrived in the area to crown a French king some five centuries earlier had the region been so excited.

The actual site chosen for the series of events was the plain of Bethany, some three miles north of Rheims. There, thousands of acres of grain fields had been cleared to construct what was called an "aeropolis"—a huge complex of grandstands, hangars, and public enclosures next to a rectangular six-mile flying course. The course was marked by tall pylons at each corner and an area in front of the grandstands designated for takeoffs and landings. Much of the flying would take place over farmland where haystacks abounded and many of the crops had not been harvested, presenting a serious obstacle to any pilot forced to put down amidst them.

"BEFORE RHEIMS THE PRACTICALITY OF FLIGHT WAS IN DOUBT. AFTER RHEIMS, IT WAS A DEMONSTRATED FACT."

Be that as it may, by the day before the meet began, the atmosphere surrounding the entire Rheims region was one of enormous anticipation. "Tomorrow . . . Sunday the 22nd," reported *Flight* magazine, "the *Grand* [*sic*] *Semaine de Champagne* will commence, and in view of the long list of prominent aviators who have promised to take part in the various contests, this will go down in history as the first great meeting of aeroplanes."

The "prominent aviators" included the most famous of the French pilots—Louis Blériot, conqueror of the English Channel, Hubert Latham, Henry Farman, Louis Paulhan, and Eugène Lefebvre. Amazingly to us

AVIATORS SEEK FAME AT GREAT RHEI

COUNT LAMBERT

LOUIS BLERIOT

HUBERT LATHAM IN HIS MONOPLANE

RENÉ DEMANEST IN HIS AEROPLANE

MAURICE GUFFROY

COUPE INTERNATIONALE D'AVIATION
FROM THE EUROPEAN EDITION OF THE N.Y. HERALD

POSTER
RHEIMS

200.000

REIMS DU 2

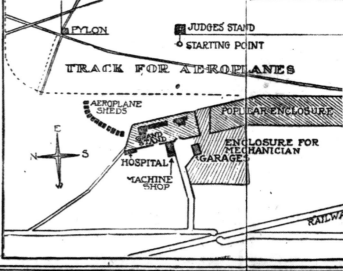

PYLON   JUDGES STAND
STARTING POINT

TRACK FOR AEROPLANES

AEROPLANE SHEDS   POPULAR ENCLOSURE

GRAND STAND   ENCLOSURE FOR MECHANICIAN GARAGES

HOSPITAL

MACHINE SHOP

RAILWAY

GENERAL PLAN OF AVIATION GRO

Glenn H. Curtiss Will Represent United States in an Effort to Bring the Exhibition and Struggle for the Trophy to This Country.

EVENING FLIGHTS WILL BE A FEATURE

NEAR the city of Rheims, France, during the last week in August will be held the world's first grand tournament for flying machines. The principal event will be the contest for the Coupe Internationale d'Aviation, a trophy and prize for which the foremost aviators of Europe and America will compete.

Other prizes have been offered for various contests calculated to demonstrate and develop the strongest features of every type of heavier than air machines. Aeronauts and scientists the world over look upon this event as providing a potent impetus to the advancement of aerial science and regard it as an occasion which will become historic as the first universal

persons a special salon has been constructed.

Electricity, gas and water have been brought to the tribunes and reception rooms. The public buffet and restaurant will be under the direction of the Hotel Castiglione, Paris. There will be seats for six hundred persons in the restaurant, and the tables are to be arranged in tiers, so that people can dine while not losing sight of the doings of the aeronauts.

For the press the committee has made elaborate arrangements. A special telegraph office has been erected, and fourteen telegraph wires will be available to flash results instantly to all parts of the world. Besides the tribunes there will be a vast enclosure 500 metres in length, for admis-

the Hempstead Plains, near Mineola, L. I., among the first a aviators, will be spre

S AEROPLANE TOURNAMENT

ROBERT ESNAULT PELTERIE

PAUL TISSANDIER

GLENN H. CURTISS AT THE WHEEL OF HIS AEROPLANE

GRANDE SEMAINE

ATION DE L

AOÛT 1909 CHAMPAGN

M. BREGUET IN HIS BIPLANE

Foremost Flying Machine Experts of Europe and America Will Compete in Historic Plains of Betheny for Prizes Covering a Wide Range of Aerial Events.

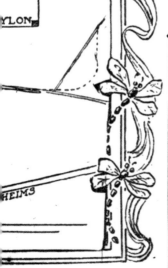

Victor, M Edouard Surcouf and M. Paul Rousseau.

The main stands are at the western end of the course, and, being directly opposite one of the short sides of the rectangle, afford a complete view of the races. They comprise private boxes and individual reserved seats, while to the right of them, within the same enclosure, is a handsome buffet so arranged that the aeroplanes can be watched while at table. To the left of the main stands are the aeroplane sheds, arranged in a semi-circular form in order that all preliminary operations can be clearly visible from the stands. Dirigible balloon sheds will be erected by the side of the aeroplane sheds. At the rear is the telegraph office, and further back a large garage for automobiles. To the right of the main stands is a vast enclosure for the general public. As the railroad from Laon the Rheims passes immediately to the rear

of the grand stands visitors from both Rheims and Paris may get off immediately at the scene of the flights.

The spherical balloon contest will take the form of a landing competition at a point fixed in advance by the commissaires, the event being open to pilots of the Aéro Club de France, with balloons of not more than 900 metres cube. Four prizes are offered, of 1,000 francs, 500 francs, 300 francs and 200 francs respectively.

For an aeronautical event of such magnitude as the Rheims meeting it has been necessary to make preparations on an unusually large scale and to prepare an aerodrome unique in the world.

It will be the first event in the history of the world to bring together all of the greatest masters of human flight, and there is little doubt that many new world records will be made.

ound of ten kilometres in the fastest

This headline said it all. The world's press was captivated by the "Great Rheims Aeroplane Tournament."

today, but perhaps not so surprising in the infant days of aviation, were the number of entrants who had little or almost no flying experience. One young man, Étienne Bunau-Varilla, had just received his airplane as a high school graduation present from his wealthy father. The entire flying experience of another competitor, known only as Monsieur Ruchonnet, consisted of one long weekend. Another participant, José Luis Sánchez Besa, was the first person from Chile ever to have taken off in an airplane. The list of those who were official entrants at the Grande Semaine, some of whom made at least one flight during the meet, includes a number of early pilots whose names have been all but lost to history. Among them were Robert Esnault-Pelterie, Andre Fournier, Jean Garbon, and two men listed only as L. Schreck and M. Fernandez. Even those fliers who had already spent many hours aloft were still encountering new sensations with almost every flight. Speaking about one of his trial runs in preparation for Rheims, Glenn Curtiss commented on a feeling that he was sure all his fellow fliers must have experienced. "I had not then become accustomed to the feeling an aviator gets," he noted, "when the machine takes a sudden drop."

[A] NUMBER OF ENTRANTS WHO HAD LITTLE OR ALMOST NO FLYING EXPERIENCE.

All told, the roster of those who were increasingly being referred to as "birdmen" was most impressive. But there were two notable absentees. The most prominent was Wilbur Wright, who had explained his absence by stating he was more interested in building and selling planes. The other was the wealthy Brazilian inventor and aeronautical pioneer, Alberto Santos-Dumont, who many in his country and throughout Central and South America believed had flown before the Wrights. Santos-Dumont had had every intention of competing at Rheims but had dropped out when a plane he was having constructed specifically for the meet failed to be completed in time.

Thirty-eight airplanes were entered in the week-long series of events. During the week before the meet, huge horse-drawn wagons, loaded with enormous crates containing disassembled air-crafts, had slowly made their way along the road from Paris to Rheims. Other dis-assembled airplanes were taken strapped in the rear

of trucks or open-backed automobiles by the pilots who would fly them. Nearly all the leading French aircraft manufacturers had planes competing in the events, including nine Voisins, four Blériots, four Henry Farmans, and four Antoinettes. Six Wright-made airplanes were also entered.

The pilots themselves came to Rheims like knights to a tournament. In keeping with the celebrity status many of them had attained, the amenities provided for them were positively extravagant. The plane manufacturers and the pilots' sponsors supplied them with fully stocked machine shops, spare parts, backup planes, trunks filled with clothing, elaborate cooking facilities, and an entourage of mechanics and helpers. Blériot, Farman, Latham, and others brought their own backup planes, spare propellers and motors, and personal helpers. Gabriel Voisin brought a full field kitchen that included a stove, pots and pans, cutlery, and his own cook and kitchen staff. In sharp contrast, Glenn Curtiss arrived with just one plane, two mechanics, and a spare propeller. At

People on a street in Rheims examine one of many signs spread throughout the city providing up-to-date information about that day's Rheims air meet events. This sign indicated wind speed and the probability of pilots being able to take to the air that day.

Rheims, it became more noticeable than ever that in these early days of flight the mechanics who tended the planes were almost as important as the pilots themselves. Although when things went well the aviators got all the praise and glory, those fliers who were most successful were the ones who understood the value of them and their mechanics work-

LA PHALANGE DE BÉTHENY

ing as a team. Pilots like Blériot and Farman recognized this and made a point of working side by side with their mechanics and also understood the importance of paying them substantial bonuses after each significant achievement.

Whatever they brought with them, and no matter how many mechanics they had, the aviators came prepared to compete in a variety of events, all of which offered rich cash prizes to winners and runners-up. The most prestigious award was the Gordon Bennett Cup, to be awarded to the pilot who completed two laps of the course in the fastest time,

Likenesses of the pilots who competed at the Grande Semaine d'Aviation de la Champagne adorned the front pages of newspapers and magazines around the world. This was the cover of one of France's leading publications.

and in doing so would be proclaimed the fastest pilot in the world. The richest cash prize (over $275,000 in today's American dollars) was to be given to the winner of the Prix de la Champagne for having made the longest single flight during the competition. Other events that promised to be hotly contested included the Prix de la Vitesse, to be awarded to the aviator who flew three laps of the course in the fastest time, the Prix de l'Altitude, won by the pilot who achieved the highest altitude, the Prix de Tour de Piste, given to the aviator who flew the fastest single lap, the Prix des Passagers, won by the flier who carried the most passengers for one lap of the course, and the Prix des Aeronauts, awarded to the pilot of the dirigible that completed five laps of the course in the fastest time.

From the beginning, what took place on the plain of Bethany was designed to be a popular festival that brought together the various social classes in a celebration of this new phenomenon: aviation. Before the festivities were over, more than one hundred twenty thousand of the more than half a million people who attended the events traveled from cities and towns in trains along a specially constructed railway line, where they disembarked at a railroad station built specifically to accommodate them. Tens of thousands of others made their way from Rheims and surrounding villages on foot or in horse-drawn wagons, where, as Robert Wohl has written, they "endured the jostling and milling crowds on the road to [Bethany] with 'cheerful eagerness.'"

This "eagerness" was evident in Rheims itself, where so many people poured into the city looking for a place to stay while they attended the meet that *every* room and almost *every* bed were occupied. Thousands, unable to find accommodation or unable to afford the inflated prices that inn- and hotelkeepers were charging, wound up staying in tents or hastily erected shelters that soon lined the road leading to Bethany.

As the ever-increasing, ever-expectant throngs made their way along

THE GORDON BENNETT CUP

NAMED FOR ITS DONOR, James Gordon Bennett Jr., the Gordon Bennett Cup was the most prestigious award in early aviation. The son of the founder, editor, and publisher of the *New York Herald*, Bennett was a man of many interests who believed in supporting worthy endeavors. During his lifetime he sponsored such projects as Henry Morton Stanley's trip to Africa to search for the lost missionary Dr. David Livingstone, Guglielmo Marconi's development of the wireless, and one of the early attempts to reach the North Pole.

James Gordon Bennett Jr.

Bennett was particularly taken with the world of sports and with those who excelled in it. "Bennett knew," said one of those close to him, "that it was sport that created the intense energy that in peace time wins races and wartime wins battles." Among his many sports-related contributions: he was behind both the first tennis match and the first polo match in the United States, and he organized the first transoceanic yacht race and won it as well.

Yet with all these considerable accomplishments he would be best remembered for the prizes he offered in three major categories—balloon racing, automobile racing, and airplane racing—and for the trophy that bore his name that was awarded to the winner of each of these events. The first of these Gordon Bennett Cups was for automobile racing and was awarded annually from 1900 to 1905. According to the rules, the race had to be held between May 15 and August 15, and it had to be a distance of between 340 and 400 miles. It was mandatory that each automobile had two side-by-side seats, one for the driver and the other for the riding mechanic.

The Gordon Bennett Cup for ballooning, the world's oldest gas balloon race, was first staged in 1906, with years off for various reasons. It is still run today and is regarded as "the premier event of world balloon racing." The basic rule of the event remains the same as when the first race was held: to fly the farthest distance from the launch site.

The Gordon Bennett Aviation Trophy was first competed for at Rheims in 1909 and was also awarded in 1910, 1911, 1912, 1913, and 1920 (the interruption was caused by World War I and its immediate aftermath). While the competition for the trophy at the 1909 Rheims meet consisted of two laps of a 6.2-mile circuit, as airplanes became faster and their engines became more dependable, the distance was increased every year. In the final year of the event, 1920, the race was held between two points that were thirty-one miles apart.

The Gordon Bennett Aviation Trophy.

The elegant restaurant at the Grande Semaine d'Aviation de la Champagne was one of the focal points of the week. It was constructed to allow patrons to have an excellent view of the contests while enjoying fine dining.

this road, they eventually came to a rise and there before them, much to their astonishment, lay not only a flying course but nothing less than a mini-city. Spread out across the plain were four huge grandstands, public enclosures, and a long line of airplane hangars. There were also barbershops, beauty parlors, shoe-shining shops, florists, telegraph offices, reception rooms, and a post office from which 50,000 postcards would be sent every day. The telephone installations were the biggest ever for a large event, with direct lines to Paris, London, Berlin, and Brussels.

At the center of it all was a huge, elegant restaurant that could seat 600 diners at a time. Decorated with electric lights shaped like pearls, it was staffed by 50 cooks and 150 waiters who prepared and served over 2,000 lavish meals a day. Spectators could dine until ten in the evening while listening to one of several orchestras. Scattered throughout the ground were bars that, before the meet was over, would serve 35,000 bottles of champagne. And it was all temporary. As soon as the meet was over, all the buildings, all the shops, everything connected to the flying course would be torn down.

The organizers had purposely done everything they could to create an atmosphere as close to that of a world's fair as possible. As one of Lord Northcliffe's friends who accompanied him to the meet stated, "An air of delightful gaiety pervaded the entire scene." To keep spectators entertained between flights, musicians, stilt-walkers, and hawkers selling toy airplanes wandered the grandstands and grounds while tightrope walkers performed overhead. Every time a French flier set a new record, one of the many bands broke into a spirited rendition of the French national anthem.

The Great Aviation Week at Rheims was particularly remarkable in that it was an enormous coming together in a spirit of jollity and inquisitiveness of people from almost every strata of society. Inside the airdrome, upper-class men and women wore elegant outfits, a stark contrast to the rest of the audience, who wore a variety of bright clothing. For even in an age of social elegance, rarely had so many of the well-known and wealthy gathered in one place as did those who were drawn to Rheims to watch the world's newest group of heroes in their first gathering together.

Before the week was over, dignitaries from around the world, including heads of state, ambassadors, former presidents, generals, admirals, and leaders of industry descended upon Rheims. Like their more humble fellow spectators, they had come to be thrilled and entertained and to be part of one of the greatest happenings of their time.

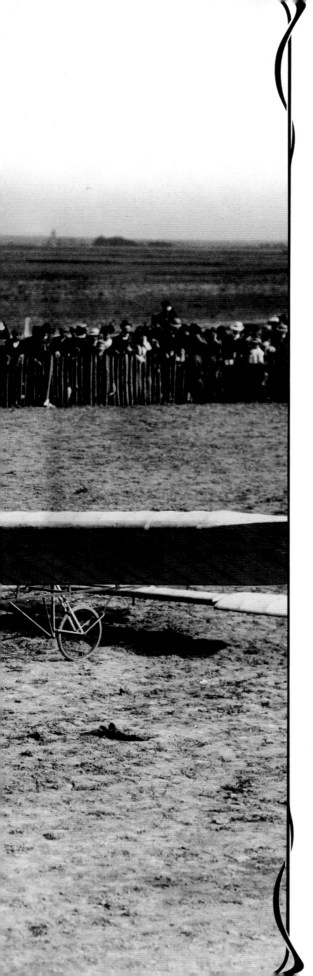

RHEIMS: DAY ONE

TORRENTIAL RAINS had been falling for days and by the time the competition was set to begin, the airdrome was a muddy quagmire. So too was the road leading to the flying grounds. Ladies' elegant shoes sank into the mud. Motorcars sank to their axles. Adding to it were the heavy winds that made flying impossible.

Yet despite it all, something astonishing was taking place. Never mind the rain and the mud and the wind, thousands of spectators arrived before opening time and began pushing against the barriers. Once let inside, those with grandstand tickets filled the seats. Soon the standing areas were also filled.

To allow spectators to follow

Bystanders look on with great interest as mechanics pull an airplane from its hangar to its takeoff position. At Rheims, spectators took advantage of every chance to get close to the competing planes.

what was taking place as effectively as possible, those in charge of the meet had created not only a scoreboard, but also a system of colored and differently shaped flags. A black flag meant that the wind was too strong for flying; a white flag signified that conditions were right for pilots to go aloft; and a red flag meant that planes were already in the air. Other flags and pennants indicated such things as which prize was at stake, which particular pilot was in the air, what the results of a particular race or contest were, and the seriousness of any accident that had just occurred.

In an age before electronic message boards, there were also signs large enough to be seen from a distance. These provided all types of information pertaining to the scheduling of the races, the participants, and directions to the various shops and dining facilities.

The first morning, the black flag was flying. But still, a spirit of optimism filled the air. The sun would come out. The miracle of flight would be revealed.

To the delight of the ever-growing throng, their optimism was rewarded. By midday flying conditions had slowly improved, and suddenly the crowd became almost hysterical as hangar doors were opened and aircraft began to appear. Each of the planes was wheeled out by its team of mechanics, but some of the spectators were so excited by their very first sight of an airplane that they rushed forward, out of the

Hauling a plane over land to its takeoff position was a necessary but often arduous task. At Rheims, it was not unusual for enthusiastic spectators to join in the procedure.

grounds and onto the field, to help bring the plane to the starting line.

The first pilot to attempt to take off was Robert Esnault-Pelterie. As he sat and waved to the crowd while his airplane warmed up, the spectators let out the greatest roar of the day thus far. But when Esnault-Pelterie attempted to move his plane, his wheels sank deep into the mud and refused to budge. When he could not get the plane out of the muck within the fifteen minutes during which all pilots were required to take off, he was ignominiously towed back toward his hangar, although even that was done to the accompaniment of cheers from the good-natured crowd.

Esnault-Pelterie's plane had hardly disappeared from view when three other pilots—Paul Tissandier, Comte de Lambert, and Eugène Lefebvre—prepared to go aloft. All three were successful, although Tissandier, who had begun his aeronautical career as a balloonist and had been taught to fly an airplane by Wilbur Wright, managed to stay airborne for only a minute. Lefebvre, on the other hand, gave the crowd its first never-to-be-forgotten moments of the meet.

As did the reporters, photographers poured into the Rheims flying grounds anxious to capture images of the action. Here a photographer snaps his pictures from inside one of the race course's pylons.

From the second he had become airborne, Lefebvre, who before the week was over would become the crowd's great favorite, left the spectators gasping with his amazing acrobatics, including sharp turns and graceful figure eights. His favorite

EUGÈNE LEFEBVRE

AT THE TIME that he participated in the Great Aviation Week at Rheims, Eugène Lefebvre, an engineer who had taught himself to fly, was the chief pilot for the French Wright Company. It was at Rheims that he earned the distinction of becoming the world's first stunt flier.

Just before competing at Rheims, Lefebvre became the first person ever to fly an airplane in Holland. Lefebvre did not win any of the coveted prizes at Rheims.

But as a widely read article in the magazine *The Aero* described, the aviator made a special and vital contribution to the success of the first-ever international air meet. Stated *The Aero*:

> Next to [Latham and Blériot], the public loved most Lefebvre, the joyous, the gymnastic. Lefebvre was the comedian of the meeting. When things began to flag . . . Lefebvre would trot out to his starting rail, out at the back of the judge's enclosure opposite the stands, and after a little twisting of propellers, his Wright Machine would bounce off the end of its starting rail and proceed to do the most marvelous tricks for the benefit of the crowd, wheeling to right and left, darting up and down, now flying over a troop of cavalry who kept the plain clear of people and sending their horses into hysterics, anon making for an unfortunate photographer who

would throw himself and his precious camera flat on the ground to escape annihilation as Lefebvre swept over him six or seven feet off the ground. Lefebvre was great fun and when he had once found that his machine was not fast enough to compete for speed with the Blériots, Antoinettes, and Curtiss, he kept to his [skill] of amusing people. The promoters of the meeting owe Lefebvre a debt of gratitude, for he provided just the necessary comic relief.

Glenn Curtiss makes a trial flight. The only American in the field, Curtiss would become a chief contender for several prizes.

tactic was to dive straight down at the grandstand and then, as men, women, and children scattered for their lives, suddenly pull straight back up. Here, on this opening day, he ascended to 300 feet, then dove to within a few feet of the ground, and then climbed back up—all while Comte de Lambert flew beneath him. As the crowd roared its approval, the equally spellbound correspondent for the newspaper *L'Intransigeant* took out his notebook and described how he and his fellow onlookers had just been treated to a glimpse at "the wonders that the near future has in store for us."

Soon the signal flags announced that the most celebrated French flier of all them all, Louis Blériot, the conqueror of the English Channel, was about to fly. Never one to ignore the crowd, Blériot first circled the field and then passed over the main grandstand, dipping one of his wings to his admirers. He completed several other circuits, each time passing over the grandstand where the crowd was now standing while cheering and waving their hats.

Blériot's wheels had hardly touched the ground when Hubert Latham's plane was hauled from its hangar. More than any other aviator at Rheims, Latham was a man on a mission. He was still bearing the emotional scars of having been beaten by Blériot in the Channel-crossing competition. At Rheims, he was out for revenge. But after flying little more than five hundred yards, his engine coughed, sputtered, started again, and then died out completely. Rather than being dismayed, the crowd cheered him mightily as he managed to glide to a smooth landing.

The highlight of the day was the competition among the French aviators, to determine which three of them would represent their country in the race for the Gordon Bennett Cup that was to take place on the near-to-last day of the meet. Indicative of the premier place that France held in the world of aviation, nine of the eleven who had indicated that they wished to compete for the cup were French. The only outsiders were George Cockburn from England and Glenn Curtiss from the United States.

Although the sun had come fully out, the wind continued to gust as high as 30 miles per hour, making it impossible for any of the French pilots to come close to flying the 12.5 miles that was the distance to be covered when the Bennett Cup race took place. Knowing that they needed to pick pilots to represent the nation in the contest, French officials in charge of that task chose Lefebvre and Blériot, who had flown better than anyone else. They also chose Hubert Latham, based solely on this reputation.

But the weather continued to improve. Before the day ended, five

Thanks to the enormous press coverage, by the end of the first day at Rheims, much of the world was becoming acquainted not only with the aviators but with their aircraft as well. (Note the creator of this illustration erroneously placed Alberto Santos-Dumont at the meet.)

L'AVIATION EN 1909
Semaine de Champagne

aviators—Tissandier, Lambert, Lefebvre, Paulhan, and Sommer—flew their circuits in the first trials of the ongoing competition for the speed prize called the Prix de Vitesse. Only seconds separated the flying times of each of these fliers, with Lambert finishing first, Lefebvre second, and Tissandier third.

By this time for the now more than 100,000 spectators, the miracle of flight had become unmistakably real. And as the day wore on, and as various aviators took to the air, the onlookers began to learn much about what to them was still an amazing new phenomenon. They were astounded by the late-afternoon flight of Belgian-born aviator Roger Sommer. Punctuated by only brief periods on the ground, his 1 hour and 20 minute demonstration showed how readily and rapidly an airplane could land and take off again.

Among the many misconceptions about flight, there had been a widespread belief that if two airborne planes passed near each other, the displacement of air that would occur would cause both aircraft to fall out of the sky. One can only imagine the gasps that came from the crowd as, in another late-day flight, Tissandier swept closely past the slower-moving Bunau-Varilla—and the audible sighs of relief when neither plane was affected by the maneuver.

On this first day, great excitement was also caused when first Tissandier and later Blériot suffered mishaps by overshooting their landings and crashing into piles of wheat sheaves in the adjoining fields. But even

A postcard showing Paul Tissandier competing at Rheims. The plane he was flying was designed by Wilbur Wright.

1133. – M. Tissandier, élève de Wilbur Wright, pilotant un aéroplane système Wright

Cet aéroplane est composé d'une cellule de 2 plans superposés ; à l'avant, gouvernail de profondeur, à l'arrière, gouvernail de direction vertical. 2 hélices marchant en sens inverse. Longueur totale 12ᵐ50. Moteur 4 cylindres 28 HP.   J. H.

these incidents failed to cause dismay when it became clear that neither pilot had been injured. Several reporters, in fact, were quick to point out how skilled the aviators had become in being able to deal with the unexpected.

The day ended in spectacular fashion. For the first time in history, seven airplanes took to the sky at the same time. The effect on the 100,000 onlookers was electric. "It seems to me that the Wright machines are writing history on the clouds," echoed England's David Lloyd George.

By the end of the first day's competition at Rheims, aviation was on the tips of more tongues than ever before. And fliers were rapidly attaining the status of heroes.

RHEIMS: DAY TWO

AS DAWN BROKE on Monday morning, it was obvious that the weather was going to be very different from the previous day. The torrential rain and gusty winds had been replaced by a bright blue sky and a gentle breeze. And at 6:00 a.m., long before any spectators began to arrive, Louis Blériot was already seated in his plane, ready to take a trial run in preparation for the day's events.

By the time Blériot took to the air, several other planes had been hauled from their hangars. Among these aircraft were several flown by pilots hoping to win the long-distance prize. For this particular contest, pilots would fly every day until the end of the

For many of those who filled the grandstands at Rheims, the spectacle of aircraft flying close over their heads would be the most amazing sight of their entire experience.

meet, and the aviator who had flown the longest distance in a single flight would be declared the winner.

There were several reasons why long-distance contests were so challenging. First of all, there was the design of the early planes. The pilot sat in the open with no protection against the wind or the rain or the cold. That was difficult enough on short flights, but on long-distance journeys, it was literally numbing. Added to this was the fact that in those early days there were no such things as aerial maps, and aerial navigation instruments were crude at best or nonexistent. There were also few wide roads that pilots could use as landmarks. The only reliable guides seen from the air were railroad tracks, and they were confusing when they split off at junctions.

Only the bravest of the early pilots became involved in long-distance flying. However, there was no question that the danger involved was a major factor in making the event so popular with spectators. This was particularly true at Rheims, where the cash prizes for the winners and runners-up of the contests were particularly high.

Among the pilots in the air almost as early as Blériot on this second day was a twenty-seven-year-old aviator who was beginning to make a mark for himself in long-distance competitions. His name was Louis Paulhan and, like many of his fellow contestants, he had only recently taught himself to fly. Born in the south of France in 1883, Paulhan had gone to sea as a young man and then joined the French army, where he served in a balloon battalion. In his spare time, Paulhan built

Long-distance flying in the first decades of the 1900s was a challenging and dangerous business. Open cockpits and lack of adequate flying instruments were but two of the factors that tested the courage and the ability of all those who attempted it.

PAULHAN FROM AEROPLANE GREETS WIFE IN BALLOON

Louis Paulhan's wife, Celeste, was an accomplished balloonist. In one of early aviation's most interesting moments, a photographer captured the scene as Paulhan in his airplane and his wife in her balloon encountered each other high in the sky.

and flew model airplanes. He became so skilled at it that in June 1902 he won a competition sponsored by the French Aero Club. His prize was an airplane built by the Voisin Company. The plane had no engine, but with the help of family and friends he was able to get one. He then taught himself to fly and, in February 1909, received a pilot's license.

Quickly establishing himself as a gifted aviator, Paulhan entered several of the earliest air shows, including the meet at Douai, France. There, just one month before the Rheims meeting, he set records for distance and duration of flight. On this bright August 23 morning at Rheims, he easily qualified for the Grand Prix de la Champagne by achieving a flight of more than 24.5 miles while staying aloft for almost an hour.

Along with witnessing Blériot and Paulhan in action, those spectators who were among the first to arrive were treated to an unexpected

Louis Paulhan was destined to become one of the most famous aviators of his day. After his participation at Rheims, he set several records and won various prizes in air meets in the United States.

sight that appeared first as a speck off in the distance and then as a long, cigar-shaped dirigible. It was the *Colonel Renard*, piloted by Henry Kapferer. Scheduled to compete with other airships later in the week in the Prix des Aeronauts, the *Renard*, with its slow, relatively silent movements, provided a dramatic contrast to the noisier, quicker planes with which it now shared the sky.

Meantime, Blériot had landed, refueled, and taken to the air again. He was now flying his successor to the Blériot XI with which he had flown the English Channel. The Blériot XII, also called the *White Eagle*, was more streamlined than its predecessor. It was also the first two-seat monoplane ever to appear. Blériot had designed and built it with one goal in mind—to win the Gordon Bennett Cup. And he was convinced that in order to do that he would have to beat Glenn Curtiss. Any doubt that he might have had about being able to do that all but vanished when, on this second flight of the day, he set a new world speed record of 42.9 miles per hour while completing the lap of the course in 8 minutes and 42 seconds. As

TO THE CROWD AT RHEIMS AND TO ALL EUROPEANS, GLENN CURTISS WAS NOTHING SHORT OF A MYSTERY MAN.

he landed to the tumultuous cheers of the crowd, Blériot could not help but be aware that Curtiss's plane was being hauled from its hangar and that the American, who had remained hidden from sight throughout the entire opening day, was at last about to take to the air. Rather than return to his hangar, Blériot decided to pick a vantage point from which he could watch his chief competitor take off and circle the course.

He was far from the only one anxious to see the mysterious Glenn Curtiss fly. Having arrived at Rheims with only the one airplane and a limited number of spare parts, Curtiss had decided to severely limit

the number of events he would enter. He would concentrate, he said, "only on such events as were for speed, and of a distance not exceeding 20 kilometers [12.5 miles], which was the course for the Gordon Bennett contest." To the crowd at Rheims and to all Europeans, Glenn Curtiss was nothing short of a mystery man.

Not so in the United States, where he had already earned a fair amount of fame. Raised in Hammondsport, a small village in Upstate New York, Curtiss was only fourteen when he quit school and, after racing bicycles at county fairs, opened his own bicycle shop. Obsessed with speed, he turned his attention to building motorcycles and racing them. Winning race after race, he became the leading motorcyclist in the nation. When, in 1907, he set an unofficial world record for a land speed of 136 miles per hour, he became known in America as "the fastest man on Earth."

It was only a short step for the nation's "fastest man" to turn to aviation. In 1908, having taught himself to fly, Curtiss, in a plane named the *June Bug* that he designed and built, won the first leg of the competition for what was known as the Scientific American trophy. As significant as the victory was for Curtiss, even more important was the fact that it was the first preannounced and publicly observed flight ever to take place in America. In early 1909, Curtiss won the second leg of the Scientific American trophy by establishing a new world record for distance flown: 24.7 miles.

Despite these accomplishments, the logical choice to represent the

Before entering the world of aviation, Glenn Curtiss was a motorcycle-racing champion. He is pictured here on the "bike" upon which he shattered several speed records.

Following pages: Curtiss became as well known for the various types of aircraft he designed as for his flying accomplishments. He is seen here piloting one of his most famous planes, the *June Bug*.

United States at Rheims was the world's most famous aviator, Wilbur Wright. But when he declined, the Aero Club of America, which had a strong influence in choosing who would represent the United States in meets, selected Curtiss. He was now thirty-one years old. Although he was extremely mild-mannered, he was also highly competitive. More than once he had told his friends, "I hate to be beaten."

At Rheims, as Curtiss knew all too well, he would be going up against the greatest fliers in Europe. He was convinced that his chance to win rested on one factor. During the short time before he needed to ship his aircraft to France, he would be able to build for his plane an engine more powerful than anything his rivals at Rheims would have in their flying machines.

As the meet drew near, Curtiss and his mechanics worked feverishly to endow his plane with the engine he felt he needed. When they were done, they had built a 50-horsepower, water-cooled motor that truly boosted Curtiss's hopes. There was, however, no time for test flights, and he had no choice but to pack up the aircraft and its engine and ship them to Paris.

Once they arrived, Curtiss, now truly racing the clock, hired a fleet of taxis to take the crates across the city to the train station for shipment to Rheims. By coincidence, Gordon Bennett himself was at the airdrome when Curtiss and his crates arrived. Having witnessed the arrival of several of the European pilots with their multiple aircraft and dozens of huge boxes of spare parts and other equipment, Bennett shook his head in disbelief, saying, "Those few packages?"

Bennett's reaction did not disturb Curtiss anywhere near as much as information he received almost as soon as he arrived in the flying grounds. "My own personal hopes lay in my motor," he later wrote. "Judge of my surprise therefore upon arriving at Rheims to learn that Blériot, who probably heard through newspaper reports that I was bringing over an eight-cylinder motor of 80 horsepower, had himself installed an eight-cylinder motor on one of his monoplanes. When I learned of this, I believed my chances were very slim indeed."

Now, with the crowd still buzzing over Blériot's record-setting flight, it was time for Curtiss to finally take to the air. Much of his despair over hearing about the Frenchman's new engine had been mitigated by encouragement from Tod Shriver, one of his mechanics who had also been with him during his motorcycling days. "Glenn," Shriver had reminded him, "I've seen you win many a race on the turns."

Curtiss's gold-winged plane was smaller than almost all the other flying machines at Rheims, and there were many in the crowd who were wondering if the never-seen-before plane would be able to fly at all. It did not take long for them to get their answer. There was an audible gasp from the crowd as Curtiss, in the plane he had nicknamed the *Rheims Racer*, rose into the

BANKING AROUND IT SO STEEPLY THAT MANY SPECTATORS WERE CERTAIN ONE OF HIS WINGS HAD TOUCHED THE GROUND.

sky and then raced for the first pylon, banking around it so steeply that many spectators were certain one of his wings had touched the ground. Rising quickly, and then briefly disappearing from sight, Curtiss roared back over the return stretch. There was an even louder gasp when the flag announcing his time was raised. Blériot's new world record for speed had lasted all of one hour. Curtiss had broken it by seven seconds, completing the 6.21-mile lap in 8 minutes and 35.5 seconds.

As for Blériot, he was hardly devastated. There were still five more days before the Bennett Cup race would take place. And he had no intention of being beaten by Curtiss again. One thing was for certain.

BIPLANE VERSUS MONOPLANE

THOSE WHO MADE their way to the flying grounds outside Rheims quickly discovered that at the time when the Grande Semaine d'Aviation took place, there were two airplane types: biplanes and monoplanes. The biplane is an aircraft with two sets of wings, an upper set and a lower set, separated by struts and wires and connected to the upper and lower parts of the fuselage. A monoplane is a fixed long aircraft with a simple main wing. Biplanes have also been called "pusher planes" because the propellers are behind the wings. Monoplanes, which have their propellers in front of the wings, have also been called "tractor planes."

For the first three decades of the 1900s, most flying machines were biplanes. The reason for this was structural. Early airplanes were extremely fragile. Because of low-powered engines and the resistance of air to planes in flight (called drag), airplanes were built of the lightest materials, such as cloth and wood. The result was that their wings could not support much weight and were thus vulnerable to wind gusts. It was because of this that most early airplanes had more than one wing.

Biplane.

There was, however, a marked disadvantage to this design. Even though biplanes were structurally stronger than monoplanes, their design produced significantly more drag than single-winged planes, making them slower. But until the beginning of the 1930s, the majority of airplane designers were willing to accept this disadvantage in return for having their plane stronger and less prone to accidents.

The person generally credited for beginning the swing to monoplanes was Louis Blériot. The extraordinary publicity that had accompanied his conquering the skies over the English Channel brought great attention to the plane he had flown. Actually, Blériot, an engineer by training, had begun experimenting with different airplane designs even before the Wright brothers' first flight at Kitty Hawk. By 1908 he had built both biplanes and monoplanes, but it was his eleventh airplane design, the Blériot XI, with which he flew over the Channel, that truly began to turn the tide toward the monoplane.

Even as early as the first air meet at Rheims, it became clear that there were those pioneer aviators, such as Alfred Leblanc, who not only preferred the monoplane, but who were already looking forward to a superior type of aircraft. Stated Leblanc:

> We haven't got to the limit of capability of the machines we now possess and we can't dream of the possibilities of new types and new motors that are certain to come. The monoplane seems to me the nearest to nature's plan, the speediest and stablest as well as incomparably the most beautiful. But I would hail the advert of a type superior to it. We shall be making long journeys over land and water in a few years.

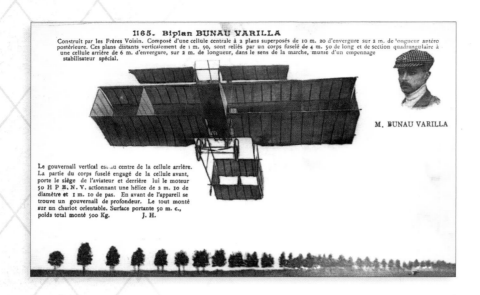

1165. Biplan BUNAU VARILLA

Construit par les Frères Voisin. Composé d'une cellule centrale à 2 plans superposés de 10 m. 20 d'envergure sur 2 m. de 'ongueur antéro postérieure. Ces plans distants verticalement de 1 m. 50, sont reliés par un corps fuselé de 4 m. 50 de long et de section quadrangulaire à une cellule arrière de 6 m. d'envergure, sur 2 m. de longueur, dans le sens de la marche, munie d'un empennage stabilisateur spécial.

Le gouvernail vertical est au centre de la cellule arrière. La partie du corps fuselé engagé de la cellule avant, porte le siège de l'aviateur et derrière lui le moteur 50 H P E. N. V. actionnant une hélice de 2 m. 10 de diamètre et 1 m. 10 de pas. En avant de l'appareil se trouve un gouvernail de profondeur. Le tout monté sur un chariot orientable. Surface portante 50 m. c., poids total monté 500 Kg.   J. H.

M. BUNAU VARILLA

Even though they were novice aviators, several of the pilots who had just begun flying became well known through their performances at Rheims. This French postcard featured Étienne Bunau-Varilla.

The quest for the Bennett Cup was shaping up to be the most anticipated air race that had ever been held.

Paulhan, Blériot, and Curtiss were not the only ones to thrill the crowd. For the second day in a row Lefebvre was in the air, delighting the spectators with his brilliant maneuvers and death-defying acrobatics. One of his special antics on this day was to circle Paulhan each time he doggedly flew around the course on his way to qualifying for the long-distance contest. And Lefebvre had an additional, more serious purpose for flying that day. He too intended to compete for the long-distance event, and he was testing a new, larger gasoline tank that he felt would give him an advantage in his quest for the prize.

Before the day was over, yet another incident caught the crowd's attention. In midafternoon, while Étienne Bunau-Varilla was in the air, gusty winds suddenly appeared. Caught in a crosswind, the aviator was blown off course. Despite battling desperately to stay aloft, he lost control of his plane and wound up in a field of oats adjacent to the flying grounds, where he surprised a far-from-delighted farmer. The only way Bunau-Varilla was able to avoid what appeared to be an imminent physical

altercation was to "turn tail" and dash out of the field. Those spectators who were watching from positions in the grandstands where they could see him cheered him on.

Despite the scares and mishaps, it had been another exciting and successful day, made evident by the fact that newspapers throughout the world were now giving front-page attention to what was taking place at the airdrome. And there was still so much more to come. The major races and contests were still days away. And there were other things to look forward to as early as the next day, when the president of France and other high dignitaries from that country, England, and the United States would be making their official visits to the meet. Rheims, the historic cathedral city, was becoming newly famous as the place where aviation was coming of age.

Many had thought that the ultimate in moving about had been achieved through the automobile. Now many were beginning to believe that a different form of transportation represented the future.

RHEIMS: DAY THREE

ALTHOUGH TUESDAY DAWNED gray and windy, there was a festive air throughout the airdrome. The highly popular president of France, Armand Fallières, was due to arrive in the afternoon. In preparation for his arrival, plants and flowers were added throughout the grounds, colorful bunting was attached to the grandstands, and the national flags of three nations participating in the meet were prominently displayed. By midmorning, although the black signal flags indicated that conditions were not yet calm enough for flying, so many horse-drawn carriages and automobiles had arrived that the sections reserved for them had been closed off

The presence of French president Armand Fallières (second from right) added a great amount of prestige to the Grande Semaine d'Aviation. He is seen here in the main grandstand, accompanied by his wife.

By the third day of the Rheims air meet, spectators had grown accustomed to seeing more than one airplane in the air at the same time. Here, Éteienne Bunau-Varilla is seen flying in the foreground while the plane in the background was being piloted by Hubert Latham.

already. The spectators stood along the rails watching mechanics working on the planes that had been lined up for President Fallières to inspect.

The gusty winds persisted until well into the afternoon. Finally, at four o'clock, the crowd that had waited all day with extraordinary patience for the flying to begin was aroused when a large squadron of cavalry galloped into the airdrome. President Fallières and his entourage were arriving. Among them were other members of the French government, a British delegation led by Chancellor of the Exchequer David Lloyd George, and two high-ranking officials from the United States Navy. The crowd, most of whom had lived through long periods of tension between France and England, was particularly taken with the way in which the officials of the two countries seemed to be getting along. Shouts of "*Vive l'Entente Cordiale*" could be heard coming from the grandstands. Later, those who had overheard the conversation these officials had while sitting in the stands reported that the main topic that was discussed was the military potential of the airplane.

The continued wait for the weather to clear also gave the president a chance to visit both the aviators and their planes. Even though neither Fallières nor Glenn Curtiss could speak the other's language, they somehow managed to "converse." A high point for the French leader came when Curtiss gave him a personal tour of the *Rheims Flyer*.

It was almost time for the presidential party to leave, but just as they were getting ready to do so the wind died down and several planes emerged from their hangars. Among the fliers most anxious to take to the air was Bunau-Varilla, fully recovered from his mishap in the field of oats and ready to make as fast a one-lap flight around the course as he could in the pursuit of the Prix de Tour de Piste. Finally spotting the all-clear flag, indicating he could take off, he not only made a creditable flight but greatly amused the crowd when, as he passed over the section of the grandstand where Fallières was seated, he yanked off his cap and waved it in a salute to the French president.

Even before Bunau-Varilla, in his Voisin aircraft, had completed his flight, the skies had darkened, the winds had risen again, and the black no-flying flag had once again been hoisted. But Louis Paulhan was set

Below: Windy conditions did not prevent Louis Paulhan from taking to the air on day three. He was determined to do so in order to honor French president Armand Fallières.

Following pages: Léon Delagrange in his airplane. At the start of the Rheims air meet, he had spent more time in the air than almost any other contestant.

GRANDE SEMAINE D'AVIATION DE LA CHAMPAGNE (Août 1909).
PAULHAN sur Biplan Voisin, Moteur Gnome, 3ᵉ Grand Prix de Champagne, 133 kil. 676 ;
3ᵉ Prix d'Altitude. 90 mètres ; 8ᵉ Prix de la Vitesse.

A DANGEROUS ENDEAVOR

IN THE EARLY DAYS of aviation, flying an airplane was one of the most dangerous of endeavors, so it was truly miraculous that, despite a number of crashes, no pilot was killed at Rheims—although it is also true that ten days after the meet had ended, both Eugène Lefebvre and Ferdinand Ferber died in crashes, and less than a year later Léon Delagrange met the same fate.

Fatalities in aviation actually began long before the first airplane was invented. In 1785, Jean François Pilâtre de Rozier, who, with a companion was the first human to fly in a balloon, was killed in a crash. In 1809, as a result of a similar tragedy, Jean-Pierre Blanchard, who with a fellow balloonist was the first to fly across the English Channel, also died.

That so many of those who made aviation history in the first decade and a half of the airplane's existence were killed while flying should not have been a surprise. As Joshua Stoff, curator of the Cradle of Aviation Museum in Garden City, New York, has written, "Even the safest planes of those pioneering days were, relative to today's [aircraft], death traps. To leave the safety of Mother Earth on those frail wings, and climb into the sky, an unexplored element into which the pioneers of flight knew they were penetrating only at great risk, demanded a unique blend of courage, dedication, curiosity and fanaticism."

This understanding of the incredible risks they were taking linked the early aviators in a special kinship. No matter which country they came from, most of them

knew each other. And because of the risks they shared, there was a genuine sense of loss among them when one of their fellow fliers was killed.

At the same time, there is no question that a sense of danger was among early flight's greatest attractions to aviators and spectators alike, a phenomenon candidly described by pioneer pilot and author André Beaumont Conneau. "[The aviator] follows a path free of any limitations," Conneau wrote. "At his pleasure, he can ascend, descend, maneuver . . . the danger? But danger is one of the attractions of flight. If man loves flying so much, it is because every step forward he makes toward the conquest of space threatens his existence."

Although amazingly no one was killed at Rheims, the meet featured several spectacular crashes. Among them was this one experienced by Louis-Charles Bréguet.

73

to take off next and he was not in any mood to obey the signal. He had been waiting all day to make a run at the Prix de la Vitesse, the three-lap speed prize. Besides that, he was a great admirer of President Fallières and he was not going to pass up the opportunity to salute his head of state. Climbing aloft and waving his handkerchief to the more than 100,000 spectators, he was greeted with a tremendous roar of approval. Then, after flying a disappointingly slow three laps around the course, he ignored the judges' order to land and began flying circles above the departing presidential party. He continued doing so all the way to the railroad station, where Fallières boarded the train back to Paris. The next day, newspapers were quick to point out that it was the first time in history that a president had received a flying escort.

ONCE AGAIN SETTING A WORLD RECORD FOR SPEED: 46 MILES PER HOUR.

Shortly after the presidential party had departed, the fickle weather changed again, the black flag was taken down, and several pilots raced aloft. Among them was Blériot, determined to post the fastest time he could in his quest for the Tour de Piste. He did it, not only posting his best time in that competition so far but once again setting a world record for speed: 46 miles per hour.

The closing movements of day three were more anxiety-provoking than exhilarating as Henry Fournier, Louis-Charles Bréguet, and Blériot, who was carrying Léon Delagrange with him as a passenger, were all involved in crashes. None of the aviators was seriously injured, but Blériot's near disaster threw a genuine scare into not only the accident-prone pilot but a group of spectators who were standing near where the crash occurred as well.

The crashes would have ended the day on a sour note but for the antics of the man who was rapidly becoming the aviator whose flying the

spectators looked forward to most. Once again, Lefebvre took to the sky and, as darkness descended, delighted the crowd with his sharp double turns, his figure eights, and other astounding maneuvers. "Lefebvre," exclaimed the *New York Times*, "came diving at the [crowd], turned in the nick of time, went sailing off, swooped down again till he made the flags on the pillars and the plumes on the ladies' hats flutter, and so played about at will for our applause." The *Times* also reported that as thrilling as Lefebvre's performance may have been, he was subsequently fined by the judges for displaying excessive "recklessness and daring."

Eugène Lefebvre at Rheims. Today he is regarded as the world's first stunt pilot.

As more and more spectators arrived at the meet by automobile, an increased number of special areas had to be set aside to accommodate them. Here, Léon Delagrange passes over the cars and their occupants as he competes in one of the events.

RHEIMS: DAY FOUR

By Wednesday, the fourth day of the meet, even the pilots who had descended upon Rheims were amazed at the way in which a seemingly unbroken stream of spectators kept pouring into the flying grounds.

Once again there was a long delay due to the weather. But when conditions improved, three fliers—Paulhan, Latham, and Fournier—prepared to take to the air. Paulhan, intent on bettering his first attempt at setting a distance record that all the other competitors in the Grand Prix de la Champagne would find impossible to beat, was the first to take off. And, having waited a considerable amount of time for the flying to

By day four, Louis Paulhan was confident that he could compete successfully with the better-known aviators at the meet. Here he is shown temporarily gaining the lead during the long-distance flying competition.

begin, the crowd greeted the sight of him in the air with cheers worthy of a conquering hero. Paulhan did not disappoint them.

Flying in wide circles, the Frenchman continually flew out of sight of the throng but then recaptured its attention each time he flew over the grandstands, where the cheering spectators rose to their feet in encouragement. Paulhan waved his hands in a return salute.

The excitement grew ever greater when the scoreboard and signal flags indicated that Paulhan was approaching Wilbur Wright's world record for long distance: 78 miles, which Wright had set the previous December. When it was announced that Paulhan had surpassed that mark, meaning that a Frenchman rather than an American now held the record, the spectators truly went wild.

Paulhan was forced to land only because he was out of fuel. When he finally set his plane down by the judges' stand, he had set the distance mark at 81 miles and the endurance record at 2 hours, 43 minutes, and 24 seconds. From the crowd, which had waited until the aviator landed, he received a welcome so loud that later many claimed the cheers could be heard all the way back in Rheims itself. Buoyed by his triumph, Paulhan used this moment in the spotlight to articulate his feelings about long-distance flying. "We must progress," he declared, "we cannot stay over one field. Cities must be linked by air as well as railroads. We must show the way."

While Paulhan was in the midst of his record-breaking flight, both Latham and Fournier had taken off. After completing one lap in an attempt at the speed record, Latham began to experience engine trouble and put down to get it fixed. Taking off again, the ever-confident flier decided that since he was in the air he might as well make an attempt at the long-distance mark. But after completing some 19 miles, engine problems once again forced him to end his flight. To the disappointment of Latham's huge legion of fans, his search for glory would have to be put off for another day.

As for Fournier, he experienced a completely different kind of adventure than did Paulhan or Latham.

"IF ALL THOSE [HAYSTACKS] HAD BEEN REMOVED," HE LATER COMPLAINED, "THIS WOULD NOT HAVE HAPPENED."

After he had completed about a half lap of the course, he also encountered problems with his engine and was forced to make a hasty landing. Unfortunately for both pilot and plane, he landed, as had Bunau-Varilla, in one of the crop-filled fields next to the airdrome, where his wheels struck a haystack, causing the aircraft to do a complete somersault before coming to a halt on its back. Luckily, Fournier was able to crawl out of

GRANDE SEMAINE D'AVIATION DE LA CHAMPAGNE (Août 1909). Glen CURTISS sur Biplan Harring Curtiss, classé : 1er dans la Coupe Gordon-Bennett, 20 kilomètres, en 15' 50" 3/5 ; 1er, Prix de la Vitesse, 30 kilomètres, en 23' 29" (Record du Monde) ; 2e, Prix du Tour de Piste, en 8' 11" 2/5.

Because he had far fewer mechanics and far less replacement parts, Glenn Curtiss limited the number of practice flights he took. He is shown here preparing for one of his rare trial runs.

the machine with only cuts and bruises, but his plane was severely damaged.

And he was outraged. "If all those [haystacks] had been removed," he later complained, "this would not have happened. We were told that all the hay would be taken away before the flying meeting started. Look at all the fields around the course, with wheat, barley, and oats cut and standing in bunches to dry. My accident might have been more serious. Someone might yet be killed."

Fournier was still standing in the middle of the field fuming when suddenly a figure on horseback appeared. It was a policeman come to check on the condition of the fallen pilot. Seeing that the aviator, while not seriously hurt, was in an unhappy frame of mind, he graciously offered the flier his mount so that he could get back to his crew and hangar.

Meantime, the spectators in the airdrome, having seen Fournier's plane go down, were holding their collective breath. Then, in one of the most unusual and surprising moments of the entire meet, a solitary figure, dressed in flying gear, came galloping into the airdrome and raced past the grandstand. As soon as the startled crowd realized that the unlikely horseman was Fournier and that he had obviously survived the crash, they once again filled the air with cheers, surpassed only by those that had greeted Paulhan, the true hero of the day.

As twilight set in, Glenn Curtiss made the surprise announcement that he was going to make an attempt to regain the single-lap-speed record that he had lost to Blériot the day before. "Give me half an hour this evening," he declared, "and I will bring the record down below eight minutes." He got his chance, and with the light rapidly fading, he took off, once again in pursuit of his chief rival's mark. But this time he came up short. After roaring into the sky, banking sharply, and giving the one-lap flight an all-out effort, he landed in 8 minutes and 11 seconds, some 7 seconds off Blériot's record. A grim-faced Curtiss, ignoring all questions from reporters, returned to his hangar. From that moment he would have only one thought on his mind—winning the race for the Gordon Bennett Cup—the contest that had brought him all the way from America.

It had been another eventful day, and even though the biggest contests of the week were still three or four days off, it was becoming increasingly clear that the biggest winner at Rheims was to be aviation itself.

A contestant at Rheims takes to the sky. The windy and often muddy conditions made almost every takeoff an adventure.

RHEIMS: DAY FIVE

AS DAWN BROKE on Thursday, both spectators and aviators became instantly aware that this fifth day promised to feature the best weather of the meet thus far. As soon as it was deemed light enough to fly, several pilots, including Latham and Delagrange, took to the air. From his expression, it was clear that Hubert Latham was a man on mission. Disappointed by his previous day's attempt at the distance record, he flew lap after lap around the course for more than an hour until his gas tank read "empty." He had flown about 40 miles, far short of the record that Paulhan had set less than twenty-four hours before. Even as Latham was landing, the disappointed aviator

Léon Delagrange was ranked as one of the leading aviators in the world. Months before the competition at Rheims, he had broken all speed records at a meet in Juvisy-sur-Orge in France.

promised himself that he would be back in the sky later that day with far better results.

Delagrange, the second man in the air, was, in many ways, typical of so many of his fellow pilots at Rheims. Not only had he been flying for a relatively short period of time, he was self-taught and, before becoming one of the world's first aviators, had distinguished himself in another field of endeavor. Delagrange, in fact, had had the most distinguished nonflying career of any aviator in his day.

Born the son of a textile worker in Orléans, France, in 1873, Delagrange demonstrated unusual artistic ability at an early age and, as a teenager, was educated at the prestigious École des Beaux-Arts. He then produced art that was shown at several galleries in Paris, and he had become particularly well-known as a sculptor, so much so that several of his works are exhibited at major galleries today, such as the Clars Gallery in Oakland, California, Hickmet Fine Arts in London, and the Robert Zehil Gallery in Monaco.

HE FLEW LOW AND CLOSE TO THE GRANDSTAND SO THAT EVERYONE IN THE CROWD COULD GET THE BEST POSSIBLE LOOK.

In 1907, Delagrange had fallen in love with flying and became one of the first men in Europe to take up aviation. He made his initial flight in April of that year after purchasing one of the early planes built by the Voisin brothers. Even though his first, 1,640-foot flight resulted in a crash upon landing, Delagrange was far from discouraged, and in September 1908, he established a distance record of 15.2 miles in 29 minutes and 53 seconds. Two months earlier, he made what is regarded as even more significant history when he gave his friend and fellow

Facing page: Aviator and sculptor Thérèse Peltier. She is popularly believed to have been the first woman airplane passenger and the first female to pilot a heavier-than-air powered aircraft.

sculptor Thérèse Peltier a ride in his plane, making this the first documented airplane ride by a woman.

On this fifth day of the meet, Delagrange, like Latham, was determined to improve on the efforts he had made thus far. Although not as daring or spectacular a flier as Lefebvre, he had nonetheless already become a crowd favorite, in great measure because whenever he could, he flew low and close to the grandstand so that everyone in the crowd could get the best possible look at him and his plane.

As he had done previously, Delagrange thrilled the crowd with his particular style of flying, but he failed to improve on any of the prize-seeking efforts he had made earlier in the week. For Latham, however, it was to be a completely different story. Ignoring the fact that the weather had deteriorated completely and both wind and rain had returned, he took to the sky in the afternoon determined to make a much better showing than he had in his morning flight. Even his strongest supporters were unprepared for the results.

The reporter for the *Indianapolis Star* wrote:

> *Latham today took glorious revenge for the hard luck which he experienced in his recent attempts to cross the English Channel, and his indefatigable but hitherto unsuccessful efforts to accomplish some notable achievement during the present meeting, by establishing a new world's record for distance . . . 95.88 miles. Latham covered . . . the full distance in 2 hours, 18 minutes and 9 seconds which is also a world's record [for endurance].*
>
> *For an hour, with fluttering wings, like a living thing, the monoplane fought its way*

against the storm of rain and wind at an average height of 150 feet, mounting higher as the wind rose, until during the worst of the storm it was up fully 300 feet. The contention of the advocates of the biplane that the monoplane would be unable to live in a strong breeze has been amply refuted.

What the reporter did not mention was that at one point in his long flight, Latham had passed over the train from Paris to Rheims and for almost two miles had raced it before easily pulling ahead.

For all in attendance, Latham's long-awaited triumph had made up for the fact that the persistent wind and rain had returned. And as late in the day as it was, there were still more thrills and spills to come. The first was supplied by George Cockburn, the only Englishman to compete at Rheims. At some 250 pounds, the heaviest competitor in the field by far, Cockburn had been the subject of concern among his

Hubert Latham's plane, the Antoinette, built for him by Léon Levavasseur, was one of the most advanced aircrafts of its day. The Latham-Levavasseur partnership was one of the most effective in early aviation history.

Léon Levavasseur

OF ALL THE NONPILOTS whose contributions were vital to the birth and growth of powered, heavier-than-air flight, no one was more important than Léon Levavasseur. Born in Cherbourg, France, in January 1863, he was short, rotund, jovial, enthusiastic—and extraordinarily talented. He was also interested in almost everything. Nothing exemplified this better than the way in which he began his schooling by studying fine arts and then abruptly switching to engineering, with a particular interest in gasoline-powered engines. Before his career was over, his inventions would include the V-8 engine, direct fuel injection, and liquid engine cooling.

Léon Levavasseur (right)
with Hubert Latham.

A visionary, Levavasseur anticipated the birth of powered flight. In 1906, with industrialist Jules Gastambide, he formed a company dedicated to manufacturing aircraft engines. At Levavasseur's suggestion, the engines were named after Gastambide's daughter, Antoinette. Within a year, most of the prize-winning speedboats in Europe were being powered by Antoinette engines.

His true passion, however, was the manufacturing of airplane engines, and by 1909, his Antoinette engines were being used by many of the pioneer flying-machine builders, including Farman, Voisin, and Blériot. But it was his association with the young, charismatic aviator Hubert Latham that would bring him his greatest fame.

During Latham's two failed attempts at being the first to fly across the English Channel, Levavasseur's smiling face and positive comments had appeared in all the leading newspapers. His enthusiasm for aviation in general and for both the airplane and the engine he had designed and built for the flier was infectious. Asked by the *Daily Mail* if he was discouraged by Latham's failure, he replied, "Not in the very least. We have proved that the Channel can be flown. A little accident to a motor, what is that? Accidents

A LITTLE ACCIDENT TO A MOTOR, WHAT IS THAT?

happen to bicycles, to horses, even to bath-chairs . . . We have a machine that can go on land, in the air, and in the water. It runs, it flies, it swims. *C'est un triomphe* [It is a triumph]!"

Levavasseur's confidence in his machine and its engine would be borne out for all the world to see at Rheims when Latham more than redeemed himself for his English Channel experience.

British supporters, who had initially feared that his ample weight would prevent his plane from getting off the ground. But Cockburn's biplane was a sturdy aircraft and he was a good pilot. Even as Latham was in the midst of his record flight, Cockburn was making his own run at capturing the distance prize. Like Latham, he too made his attempt more exciting by racing and beating a passing train. But, like almost all the contestants for the Grand Prix, his flight fell short when he ran out of fuel.

The Comte de Lambert had been the only other flier besides Latham and Blériot to have seriously considered making an attempt to fly the English Channel. On this day, lost in the excitement of Latham's long-distance achievement, was how close Lambert came to surpassing

The ongoing long-distance competition was one of the most popular attractions at Rheims. Here, spectators cheer on Hubert Latham as he competes for the coveted prize.

his rival's mark. When Lambert finally ran out of fuel and was forced to land, he had been in the air for nearly 2 hours and had covered more than 72 miles.

It had been a memorable day, one that drew to a close on a couple of anxious notes. First, Henri Rougier came close to what could have been a major disaster when, after completing one lap of the course, his engine stalled as he was flying directly over one of the public viewing enclosures. With his plane plunging quickly downward and spectators scattering in all directions, Rougier somehow managed not only to put down in the only open space in the enclosure but also to escape serious injury.

The day actually ended with another accident, this one suffered by none other than Louis Blériot. As the only pilot to have a plane equipped

with two passenger seats, he was a strong favorite to win the passenger-carrying contest that would take place on the next-to-last day of the meet. At 6:40 p.m., he was practicing for that event by conducting a trial flight with a passenger aboard known only as Mr. Roth. Flying low in order to ease Roth's fears, Blériot suddenly experienced trouble with his steering gear. He immediately headed for the landing area, but just as he was about to put down, a squadron of mounted soldiers appeared directly in his path. Swerving to avoid them, he crashed into a fence, powered through it, and came to a halt. Although the undercarriage and the wheels of the airplane were damaged, neither pilot nor passenger was injured. Indicative of the esteem in which Blériot was held, shouts of "Viva Blériot!" rang through the air as he emerged from the wreckage.

RHEIMS: DAY SIX

FOR AVIATORS and spectators alike, Friday, August 27, 1909, was a very special day. It was the final day to compete for the Grand Prix de la Champagne that by now, especially after Hubert Latham's flight, newspapers were billing as "the greatest race of all time." The crowd was growing so large that those arriving in automobiles after 9 a.m. were finding it impossible to find a place to park. It was inconceivable that Latham's distance record of 95.88 miles would be broken. Certainly not just one day after it had been set!

As for the aviators, many of them and their mechanics had spent much of Thursday night making adjustments to their

By day six, the quest for the long-distance prize had come down to a spirited competition between Farman, Paulhan, and Latham. At one point it appeared that Paulhan, shown here temporarily setting a distance record, would be the winner.

planes—replacing engines, rebuilding wing structures, replacing propellers with, hopefully, better ones.

With the wind virtually at a standstill, many of the pilots were anxious to make an early final attempt at the prize. One of the first was Paulhan, who only two days before had held the lead in the contest. But this was not to be his day. He had barely taken off when suddenly he saw Léon Delagrange's plane coming out of a turn and heading straight for him. Reacting quickly, Paulhan dropped his airplane's nose in order to avoid a collision—but the downdraft from Delagrange's plane pushed him farther downward and one of his wings hit the ground, causing him to crash. Although badly shaken, Paulhan escaped with only cuts to his nose and hand, but his quest for the Grand Prix was over.

Other aviators endured mishaps. Tissandier and Sommer had taken off in rapid succession. But each had suffered mechanical problems, particularly with their engines, and each was forced to call it quits for the day.

Farman was now in the sky alone. In a bold and risky move, he and his mechanics had arisen before dawn and installed a new type of motor in his plane: a 50-horsepower air-cooled Gnome rotary engine. He had not had time to adequately test the new power plant, but so far it was performing perfectly during his flight that day. As far as Farman was concerned, the engine had to. Unlike most of his competitors, this was his one and only attempt at winning the Grand Prix.

On and on Farman flew, endlessly circling the course. Each time he passed over one of the grandstands the spectators jumped to their feet and cheered him mightily. Two hours into his flight he broke Wilbur Wright's distance record; the same one that Latham had shattered. A half hour later, and three-quarters of an hour before darkness was due to set in, Farman surpassed the record that Latham had set only the day before.

And still he flew on, well after it began to get dark. "The closing laps of that flight," one of the spectators later wrote, "extending as they did into the growing of the dusk, made a breathlessly eerie experience for such of the spectators as stayed on to watch—and these were many. Night came on steadily and Farman covered lap after lap just as steadily, a buzzing, circling mechanism with something relentless in its isolated persistency." The later it got, the colder it got, and as he sat unprotected on the lower wing of his biplane *with* the frigid wind beating against him, Farman began to feel numb. But *still* he flew, his way lighted by

THEY PUT THEIR WATCHES AWAY AND LEFT. BUT THAT DID NOT STOP FARMAN.

THE WRISTWATCH

THERE ARE MANY THINGS, large and small, that owe their popularity to the birth of the airplane. One of these is the wristwatch.

As the 1900s began, one of the most recognizable names in aviation was Alberto Santos-Dumont, the man who, although born and raised in Brazil, was in love with Paris. One of Santos-Dumont's ambitions was to become a celebrity in his adopted city, and he succeeded in doing so by making the first-ever dirigible flight around the Eiffel Tower.

As he frequented Paris's most elegant cafés and restaurants, Santos-Dumont often dined with a well-known Parisian resident named Louis Cartier. He and his two brothers were the grandsons of early watchmaker Louis-François Cartier, who, in 1847, had started a small jewelry store. Under the three grandsons' ownership the store grew to the point that by 1900 Cartier had become not only highly successful, but one of the great names in the world of jewelry.

In 1904, after one of his flights over Paris, Santos-Dumont was dining with Louis Cartier at the famous restaurant Maxim's when he complained to his friend that the pocket watch he carried with him on his flights was useless. While flying, he had to keep both hands on the controls at all times and could not do so while trying to get at his pocket watch.

The conversation inspired Cartier to design a flat watch with a strap that fit neatly on Santos-Dumont's wrist, enabling him to check the time of his flight without letting go of the controls. It was actually not the world's first wristwatch: another jewelry company, Patek Phillipe, is credited with having invented the first one. But because of Santos-Dumont's popularity and fame, it was Louis Cartier's creation that became popular, first with other aviators and then with the public at large.

Today, the Cartier company remains one of the most famous jewelry and watch manufacturers and sellers in the world. And it still markets a line of Santos-Dumont watches, the most popular being the Cartier Santos 100 Carbon watch.

Early Cartier wristwatch.

automobile head lamps that had been switched on to help him stay the course.

At 7:30 p.m., the judges announced that it had gotten so dark they could no longer time him. They put their watches away and left. But that did not stop Farman. Knowing that he still had about three gallons of fuel in his tank, he made one more wide lap around the course before coming in for a perfect landing.

He had done it. Not only had he established a new distance record, set officially at 116 miles, and a new endurance record of 3 hours, 4 minutes, and 56 seconds, it was also obvious that if the judges had not stopped timing him, the marks would have been much higher. He was almost totally numb with cold but, as the London *Times* reported, "was seized upon by the enthusiastic crowd and carried in triumph to the restaurant where a scene of almost delirious excitement was witnessed." At the same time, musicians, in recognition of Farman being half French and half English, broke into the national anthems of both countries.

On hand to officially congratulate Farman was France's minister of public works, Alexandre Millerand, who would later serve as both president and prime minister of his nation.

Finally rescued from the adoring throng, Farman was carried to his hangar by his mechanics, where he gave his only interview to a crowd that was getting larger every minute.

Asked to describe how cold he had felt, Farman replied:

Cold . . . I was almost frozen. I had put on three woolen jackets, one over the other, and two pairs of socks. I was still cold, but I dared not stop. I had to keep going as long as the engine kept going. The engine ran better at lower altitude so I kept as low as I dared. I had only sixty-three

Facing page: Henry Farman wins the long-distance competition in his Voisin-built airplane. During his flight, Farman repeatedly swooped down almost to the ground, and then flew off into the distance before returning.

The Rheims Triumvirate

THE THREE MEN WHO HAVE PROVED THE FEASIBILITY OF LONG-DISTANCE FLIGHT

Latham
Who flew 96 miles in 2hrs. 18mins.
Second in the Grand Prix

Farman
Who flew 116 miles in 3hrs. 4mins.
Winner of the Grand Prix

Paulhan
Who flew 81 miles in 2hrs. 43mins.
Third in the Grand Prix

FARMAN MAKING HIS RECORD FLIGHT OF 116 MILES AT RHEIMS

The great competitions at Rheims have proved the improbable. That such feats as those of Paulhan, Latham, and Farman would be achieved so soon after the earlie-t efforts was never dreamed by the most sanguine. The progress of aviation is admitted to equal that of automobilism itself, and to-day we see the aeroplane a practical means of locomotion. In a few years, flight will be in vogue all over the country, and to fly will be one of the commonplaces of daily life

Below: The Grande Semaine d'Aviation de la Champagne attracted more than two hundred thousand spectators from all classes of European society.

Facing page: By the end of day six, artists had joined photographers in celebrating the triumph that the Grande Semaine d'Aviation de la Champagne had already become. The creator of this fanciful drawing emphasized his point by placing twelve airplanes in the air at the same time.

liters of gasoline but I was determined to stay up until it had all gone. My luck has turned and I have won the only race I really wanted to win.

The final competition for the Grand Prix de la Champagne had been the only major event of the sixth day of the Great Aviation Week at Rheims. Immediately ahead were two days during which many of the most important competitions would be held and many more prizes would be awarded. But Farman's remarkable achievement and his competitors' noble efforts had made day six a thrilling and unforgettable experience.

REIMS — Grande semaine d'aviation
La Grande Tribune

RHEIMS: DAY SEVEN

FOR THE TENS of thousands who had made the trek to Rheims, Friday had been a day of great excitement. And Saturday promised to offer even more. At the top of the list was the race for the Gordon Bennett Cup, the most publicized and highly anticipated event of the entire meet. Once again, well before the events began, the grandstands and public enclosures were filled almost to capacity with spectators anxious to witness a race they had been reading about for weeks.

As far as most of them were concerned, there were still only two heavy favorites to win the race. As skilled and daring as they might be, none of the other aviators seeking the Bennett Cup

An airplane manufacturer as well as a pilot, Glenn Curtiss made many of his own repairs on his aircraft. Here, prior to the Bennett Cup race, he makes important alterations to his engine.

had anywhere near the reputation and talent for speed as did Louis Blériot and Glenn Curtiss. The experts agreed.

Curtiss had been up since before dawn working with his mechanics, testing *every* wire, *every* bolt, and *every* other part large and small in his *Rheims Flyer.* When he was satisfied that all was in order, he notified the judges that he was ready to make a test run and that he wanted it to count as an official attempt to win the one-lap Prix de Tour de Piste. "As conditions were apparently good," Curtiss would later write, "I decided to make my trial flight shortly after ten o'clock. The machine was brought out, the engine given a preliminary run, and at half past ten I was in the air . . . I climbed as high as I thought I might . . . so that I might take advantage of a gradual descent throughout the race, and thus gain additional speed . . . I cut the corner as close as I dared and banked the machine high on the turn." He was now about to enter

Glenn Curtiss attempts to earn the speed prize named the Prix de Tour de Piste.

the backstretch of the course and make as fast a run as he could for the finish line. But entirely without warning he ran into an invisible wall of turbulence. "The shocks were so violent," he recalled, "that I was lifted completely out of my seat."

At this point, Curtiss had two choices. He could either ease up on his throttle and hope to gain control of his plane, or he could try to power his way through the turbulence. The furthest thing from a daredevil aviator, Curtiss nonetheless decided to power his way through. And it worked. Despite another period of violent shaking, he was able to regain smooth air and make a safe landing.

"THE SHOCKS WERE SO VIOLENT," HE RECALLED, "THAT I WAS LIFTED COMPLETELY OUT OF MY SEAT."

To his total surprise, as soon as his wheels came to a stop he was mobbed by a group of jubilant fellow Americans. A quick glance at the huge scoreboard next to the landing area gave him his explanation. Despite the frightening stretch of turbulence, he had set a new world record for speed.

Back in his hangar, a still-stunned Curtiss tried to figure out what had happened. And slowly the answer came to him. He had not set the speed record *in spite* of the turbulence he had encountered, but *because* of it. The more he thought about it, the more he remembered how, during the few trial flights he had taken earlier in the week, he had noticed and had been surprised by the fact that because there had been so much rain in the area, the terrain at Bethany, as it was drying out, released pockets of updrafts that resurfaced in the type of turbulence he had experienced. Most important, he realized, these updrafts, when they occurred, helped increase the speed of planes flying through them. "I thought the matter over," he later recounted, "and came to the conclusion that this disturbed condition of the atmosphere without any wind was most conducive to speed . . . With the broken air currents the propeller always had a fresh mass of air to work on, consequently obtaining great push."

It was a startling revelation. Curtiss knew that if he was to take advantage of it and increase his chances of winning the Bennett Cup, he had to act rapidly before the conditions he had just experienced disappeared.

He notified the judges immediately that he was about to make the one and only two-lap run for the Gordon Bennett Cup that each contestant was allowed. Curtiss later explained:

> We hurriedly filled the gasoline tank, gave the machine a final checking, and spun the propeller. Being far back from the takeoff line, I got the machine quickly off the ground and climbed as high as I could before passing the judges' stand below me. With the nose of the machine pointing down sufficiently to gain more speed, I headed for the far end of the field. The throttle was wide open, it was my only chance. I banked steeply as I turned toward the "rough" part of the course.
>
> The air was wild. It seemed to be tearing at the wings. . . . There was nothing else now but to keep the throttle fully open and head for the final turn. It was all or nothing.

For the spectators, Curtiss's second lap around the course was even more amazing to behold than his first-lap maneuvers. Using the unique skills he had developed as a motorcycle driver, he banked more sharply at every pylon than anyone in the crowd had ever seen. Still more astounding, he did so without dropping a bit of speed. As he headed for the finish line, the air seemed to drop out from under him as he passed above the "graveyard" where, as he noted, "so many machines had gone down and were smashed during the previous days of the meet."

When he landed, Curtiss was once again mobbed by his American supporters, made

CURTISS'S SECOND LAP AROUND THE COURSE WAS EVEN MORE AMAZING TO BEHOLD THAN HIS FIRST-LAP MANEUVERS.

even more ecstatic by their knowledge that this had been no test run; this was an attempt to win the most prestigious aviation prize in the world. The cheers got even louder when Curtiss's time for the two circuits of the course was announced at 15 minutes and 50.6 seconds. He had completed the first lap in 7 minutes and 57.6 seconds. He had finished the second lap in 7 minutes and 53.5 seconds, at a speed of 46.5 miles per hour. That was faster than any person had ever flown through the air!

It was a magnificent performance, and Curtiss was well aware of it. But he was not as confident as his fans that the Bennett Cup would definitely be his. The other competitors, including the legendary Blériot, were yet to fly. And until they did, he said, he would never allow himself to believe that he had won.

The next competitor to fly was England's George Cockburn. But after completing one lap, he experienced engine trouble and was forced to make an emergency landing in a field where, for the second time in the meet, he collided with a bale of wheat. Fortunately, he was once again unhurt.

With Curtiss and Cockburn having flown, the enormous crowd,

aware that the three remaining contestants were all French, came fully alive. The first of these fliers was the enormously popular Lefebvre. And for the first time in the meet the flamboyant aviator was sporting a deadly serious demeanor. Fully aware that this was no occasion for stunts or daredevil antics, he gave it his best effort and completed both laps. But his plane was simply not fast enough to challenge the time that Curtiss had posted. If, on this day, a Frenchman was going to win the Gordon Bennett Cup, it would have to be either Latham or Blériot.

It would not be Latham. Taking off in the afternoon after activities had paused for lunch, he posted an excellent time on his first circuit around the course. But in his second lap, his plane, much larger than Curtiss's, was slowed down considerably by the turbulence he encountered, and he finished almost two minutes behind the American. France's hopes for the prized trophy now rested solely with Blériot.

But it was almost five o'clock and the crowd, under the impression that all racing had to stop at five, was growing increasingly restless. Did this mean that after waiting all day they would not get to see their hero Blériot outdo the American? But the mood of the airdrome changed abruptly when, to the accompaniment of almost deafening cheers, Blériot and his plane emerged from his hangar. France's greatest aviation hero was ready to claim aviation's greatest prize.

And it certainly appeared that he was about to do just that. Taking off with a confident quick wave to his followers, he completed the first lap of the course with such obvious speed that those in the grandstands rose to their feet in acclaim. And they became absolutely delirious when Blériot's official time for the lap was announced. He had beaten Curtiss's first lap time by a full 4 seconds.

As Blériot began his second circuit of the course, Curtiss looked on from the back seat of an American friend's automobile. As much as he had staked everything on winning this one race, he could not help

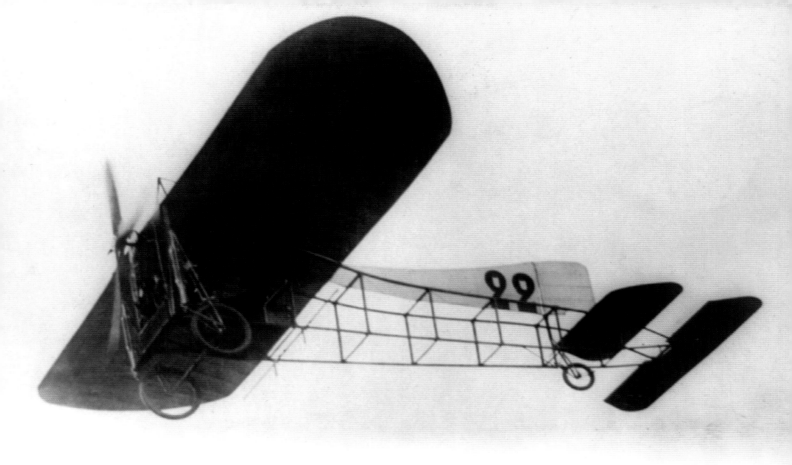

admiring Blériot's skill in handling his large monoplane. "He started off at what seemed to be a terrific burst of speed," Curtiss would later state about Blériot's flight. "It looked to me just then as if he must be going twice as fast as my machine had flown; but it must be remembered that I was very anxious to have him go slow. The fear that he was beating me was father to the belief."

As Blériot was starting his second lap, it certainly seemed as if he was maintaining the same blistering speed. Though to a few of the most astute observers, it did seem that as he fought his way through the turbulent area his plane did swing a tiny bit off course. Landing to the loudest cheers of the day, Blériot acknowledged them as he jumped down and ran over to the timekeeper's hut to get his official results.

As for Curtiss, he was preparing himself for what he believed was the

Louis Blériot during his gallant attempt to win the Gordon Bennett Cup. The mostly French crowd was shocked when, by the smallest of margins, he finished second to Glenn Curtiss.

inevitable—the news that Blériot had won. "I confess," he later wrote, "that I felt a good deal like a prisoner awaiting the decision of a jury. I had done my best and had got the limit of speed out of the machine; still I felt that if I could do it all over again I would be able to improve on the time."

But then something totally unexpected happened. The seemingly endless cheering that had erupted from the moment Blériot had landed suddenly stopped. It was as if someone had shut off a terribly loud recording so abruptly that Curtiss sat dazed with absolutely no idea what had happened. "I sat in Mr. Bishop's automobile, wondering why there was [suddenly] no shouting," Curtiss would later write, "when I was startled by a shout of joy from my friend Mr. Bishop who, [*sic*] had gone over to the judges' stand. 'You win! You win!' He cried, all excitement as he ran toward the automobile. 'Blériot is beaten by six seconds!'" Glenn Curtiss had entered the history books by winning the most important airplane race just held.

Like the winning racehorse after a major derby, Glenn Curtiss's plane is paraded before the grandstands. Curtiss's triumph would not only bolster his status as a pilot but would be a boon to his aircraft-manufacturing business.

Still dazed, Curtiss was led by his admirers to a flagpole where a huge American flag was slowly being raised. At the same time, an almost silent French crowd was "treated" to the playing of the "The Star-Spangled Banner." Within twenty-four hours, headlines in newspapers around the world would hail Glenn Curtiss as "Champion Aviator of the World." Meantime, Curtiss would report that "Blériot himself, good sportsman that he is, was among the first to extend congratulations to America and me personally." Curtiss would add that "there was a reason beyond pure patriotism why [my countrymen] felt so happy over the result [of the race]. It meant that the next international race would be held in the United States and that the best foreign machines would have to come across the ocean to make a try for the Cup the following year."

Given the excitement engendered by the Bennett Cup race, it would not have been difficult to lose sight of the fact that there was still more to come on this next-to-last day of the meet. And little more than half an hour after the Blériot-Curtiss duel had ended, the grandstands and their viewing areas came alive again as an event that had a very special bearing on the future course of aviation, the Prix des Passagers, got underway. Because of the fragile nature of the airplanes of the day, there were only two competitors for the prize, Farman and Lefebvre.

Originally there had been a third entrant, Louis Blériot. And because he had the only plane that had seats for two passengers, he had been

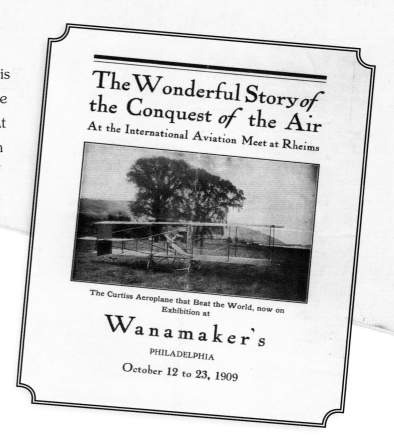

The Wonderful Story of the Conquest of the Air

At the International Aviation Meet at Rheims

The Curtiss Aeroplane that Beat the World, now on Exhibition at

Wanamaker's

PHILADELPHIA

October 12 to 23, 1909

Wanamaker's, one of the United States's largest department stores in the early twentieth century, was quick to capitalize on the great victory by an American aviator. The establishment proudly announced that it was putting Curtiss's airplane on display for all to see.

Henry Farman in his plane with a passenger. When he succeeded in carrying two passengers, he won the Prix des Passagers event.

regarded as the favorite to win the prize. But after failing to capture the Gordon Bennett Cup, Blériot became more determined than ever to win the one remaining speed contest, the Prix de Tour de Piste. To give himself the best chance, he had removed the passenger seats and had withdrawn from the passenger-carrying event.

With the Marquis de Polignac riding along as his passenger, Farman was the first in the air in the quest for the Prix des Passagers. Flying smoothly, he completed the course in 9 minutes and 52 seconds. As soon as he landed, Lefebvre took off, carrying the famous sculptor Herbert Ward with him. More affected by the turbulence he encountered than Farman had been, he completed the course in a slower 10 minutes and 39 seconds. The prize, however, was to be awarded not for time elapsed but for the largest number of passengers carried. And by going aloft again, this time with two newspapermen on board, representing an additional 292 pounds, Farman became the proud winner of the Prix des Passagers.

The excitement was still not over. Just as the crowds were beginning to leave, Blériot and his mechanics were seen bringing the Blériot XII out of its hangar. He was about to make his attempt to capture the Prix de Tour de Piste trophy. In a fitting end to a day that few of the spectators would ever forget, Blériot took to the air and completed a lap of the course in a sizzling 7 minutes and 47 seconds. Once again, he and Curtiss had exchanged places as the holder of the right to be called "the world's fastest man."

Throughout the Rheims air meet, Louis Blériot remained extraordinarily popular with the enormous French crowds. Here he is mobbed after winning the speed prize named the Prix de Tour de Piste.

GRANDE SEMAINE D'AVIATION DE CHAMPAGNE (Journée du 26 Août)
L'appareil de Blériot s'abat devant les Tribunes

RHEIMS: DAY EIGHT

AS THE GATES OPENED for the final day of the meet, press and public alike could only shake their heads in wonder at the more than 250,000 people who were piling into the flying grounds. It probably should not have been a surprise that this last day would draw the largest crowds of the week. Glowing accounts of the previous day, particularly the breathtaking contest between Curtiss and Blériot, had made the front pages of newspapers almost everywhere.

With things drawing to a close, many of the newspapers were also featuring reflections on the meaning of the meet by the aviators

The photographer who created this montage labeled it "The Sport of the Future: A flock of aeroplanes in flight at Rheims." He might more accurately have called it "the future of transportation."

themselves, including an interview given to the *New York Times* by Henry Farman. He stated:

> When we have had a month or two to think over the results of this meeting, we shall be better able to talk of the future of the aeroplane. . . . When one considers that an art so new is represented here by a score of men and nearly twice as many machines, it makes one wonder what will be able to assemble here or elsewhere next year even. We are going on and on—feats that were thought preposterous to imagine are now easily accomplished. . . . I look for results that will astonish the public very soon even more than they have been astonished.

Louis Blériot had long been known for the many accidents he had experienced. The crash he suffered during the last day of the Rheims meet was among his most spectacular.

Actually, the quarter of a million who had packed into the grandstands and public enclosures were not going to have to wait until "next year" to be astounded. Before the day was over, they would be eyewitnesses to two of the most exciting events of the entire meet: the final phases of both the Prix de l'Altitude and the Prix de la Vitesse.

The conditions on this final day were perfect for flying and record-breaking. And one of the events where records seemed most likely to fall on this last day was in the final competition for the Prix de la Vitesse. The race between Curtiss and Blériot for the Gordon Bennett Cup had convinced the aviation world that the final attempts for the three-lap speed contest would once again come down to a competition between the American and the Frenchman and that it would be just as hotly fought a duel. The fact that only a day ago the lead in the one-lap speed race had once again changed hands between the two men added to this conviction.

But it was not to be. As he took to the sky and began his assault on the coveted speed prize, Blériot appeared to be in complete control of his plane. But suddenly it became obvious that something had gone terribly wrong. To the crowd's horror it was clear that he was heading frantically back to earth in an attempt to make a forced landing.

What had happened was that Blériot's propeller had splintered, resulting in a violent vibration that

Following pages: Less than twenty-four hours after winning the Gordon Bennett Cup, Glenn Curtiss concluded his flights at Rheims by winning another prize. He is shown here as he establishes the fastest time in the three-circuit speed contest named the Prix de la Vitesse.

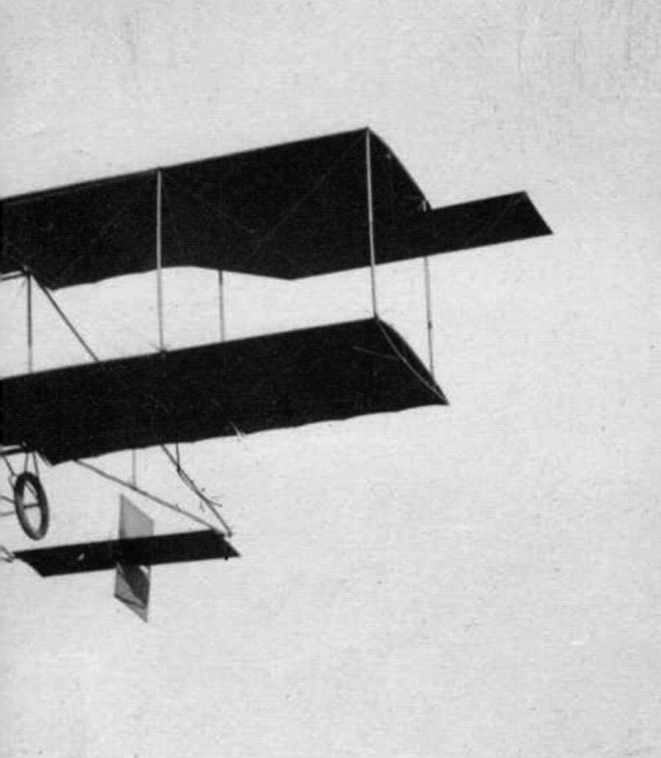

Dirigibles

THE PRIX DES AERONAUTS was designed to remind the public of a flying machine that had first made its appearance long before the airplane. Airships, commonly called dirigibles, from the French word *diriger*, to direct or steer, were the first aircraft capable of controlled, powered flight.

A dirigible is characterized by a gas-containing elongated body called its envelope and by a gondola suspended beneath the envelope, which carries its crew and passengers. A dirigible's engines are also usually mounted in the gondola.

The world first became aware of the possibility of dirigibles in 1670 when the Jesuit priest Francesco Lana de Terzi, whom some have called the "father of aeronautics," published a depiction of what he called an aerial ship that was held aloft by four copper spheres. During the 1700s and early 1800s individuals around the globe, many of them hot-air balloonists, attempted to develop a dirigible capable of making an engine-powered flight. That vital breakthrough came in 1852 when Frenchman Henri Gifford flew about twenty miles in a powered airship.

The next great breakthrough came in July 1900 when a dirigible built by German count Ferdinand von Zeppelin made its first flight. The series of dirigibles that he designed was the strongest that had ever been constructed (von Zeppelin also piloted many of them), and they became the most acclaimed dirigibles in history.

Just one year after the first Zeppelin flight, another dirigible and its designer/pilot also made headlines when, on October 19, 1901, Alberto Santos-Dumont flew over Paris in the latest of the many airships he created. His flight included a loop around the Eiffel Tower.

Santos-Dumont's widely reported feat spawned a host of airship flights by other aviators. Among them were two failed attempts to fly a dirigible to the North Pole.

As was the intention of the organizers of the Rheims air meet, the Prix des Aeronauts competition, witnessed by such an enormous gathering of spectators, did much to remind the public of the presence of the airship. And despite the continual phenomenal development of the airplane, dirigibles remained an important part of the aviation world into the 1930s.

An early dirigible.

threatened to tear his aircraft apart. Racing toward earth, he fought to take the plane out of its dive but before he could do so, one of its wheels and one of its wings hit the ground, and it crashed nose downward. Then the gasoline tank exploded. Flames shot up and Blériot was seen emerging from the wreckage with his clothing on fire.

As officials, policemen, reporters, photographers, and spectators rushed to his aid, Blériot put the flames out by rolling on the ground. But along with the burns, he had wounds to his forehead, shoulder, and hands. Fortunately, none of the injuries were life-threatening, but Blériot was certainly through flying for the day and for the rest of the meet.

FLAMES SHOT UP AND BLÉRIOT WAS SEEN EMERGING FROM THE WRECKAGE WITH HIS CLOTHING ON FIRE.

With his chief rival out of contention, Curtiss had only Latham and Tissandier as serious challengers. And when it was his turn to fly, he removed any doubt as to what the outcome would be by completing the three laps in an amazing time of 25 minutes and 29 seconds. Latham finished second and Tissandier wound up third.

As for Blériot, he received a large measure of consolation when it was determined that throughout the week it was he who had flown the fastest single lap around the course, making him the winner of the Prix de Tour de Piste. But his latest mishap would have a major effect on him. For the man who, while becoming one of aviation's greatest heroes, was also known for the extraordinary number of crashes he had experienced, it was one crash too many. Gradually, he retired from racing and concentrated on his airplane-manufacturing business

Meantime, the rest of the final day's events went on. In sharp contrast to the high drama and excitement of Latham's victory in the

Facing page: Spectators cheer as one of the contestants in the Prix de le Vitesse flies overhead. Like all the speed contests, the event was a huge crowd favorite.

altitude contest and Curtiss's triumph and Blériot's crash in the Prix de la Vitesse, now was the Prix des Aeronauts, a five-lap speed trial for dirigibles. Actually, "speed" was hardly the word for the slow-moving airships. By the time the event was held, only two contenders were ready to take part. The winner of the contest, in a time of just over 1 hour and 19 minutes, was the French army dirigible *Colonel Renard.* The loser was the *Zodiac,* flown by Comte Henry de la Vaux, a cofounder of the French Aero Club and the man responsible for having suggested Rheims as the site of the world's first international air meet.

NOTHING HAD ASTOUNDED THE ONLOOKERS MORE THAN THE SIGHT OF BOLD PILOTS CLIMBING HIGHER AND HIGHER.

With the winners of the Prix de la Vitesse, the Prix de Tour de Piste, and the Prix des Aeronauts determined, there was only one event remaining to complete the day and the meet as a whole. It was no accident that the organizers had scheduled the final competition for the altitude prize to be the gathering's very last event, the one that would be freshest in the minds of the spectators as they departed. During the week, nothing had astounded the onlookers more than the sight of bold pilots climbing higher and higher until they became rapidly disappearing specks in the sky. Now, with Paulhan, Farman, Latham, and Rougier ready to pursue a prize one last time, the enormous crowd was ready for yet another record, and a most important one, to be set.

Despite giving it their best efforts, both Paulhan and Rougier failed to attain an altitude that would give them a reasonable chance to win the prize. But the crowd truly came to life when Farman roared into the air. Could he add the altitude trophy to the distance record he had set earlier? It certainly looked like he would as he stunned the immense gathering by climbing higher and higher in three great spirals, each about a mile in diameter, until he reached the astounding height of 360 feet.

As Farman headed back down, the entire airdrome resounded with a gigantic roar. Much of it was in acclaim for what Farman had just accomplished. But part of it was also because another huge crowd favorite, Hubert Latham, had just taken off in search of the prize. Would Latham finally win the great award at Rheims that he so eagerly sought? Or, as had happened in the distance contest, would he finish second to Farman again?

Rising relentlessly upward, Latham and his Antoinette VII kept climbing until it became obvious to the spectators that he was surpassing the height that Farman had attained. Something else was obvious as well. As he flew ever upward in leisurely circles, Latham was treating the crowd to one of the most graceful flights anyone in the huge throng had ever seen.

Describing what she witnessed as Latham took to the air, author and former balloonist Gertrude Bacon wrote:

> A sudden, mighty rush and into the air plunged another bird—but such a bird!—a fierce hawk or better [yet], a dragonfly—a darting, graceful, immensely powerful dragonfly, instilled with the true beauty of flight, with boundless reserves of strength and speed, steady as a rock, graceful exceeding with its long shapely body and its single pair of outstretched wings. "Latham, Latham!" shrieked the ecstatic crowd, waving hats and handkerchiefs and programs in wild applause.

WINNERS OF THE GRANDE SEMAINE d'AVIATION

Grand Prix de la Champagne

PLACE	PILOT	MAXIMUM DISTANCE FLOWN Kilometers	Miles	TIME
1	Farman	180	116	3:04:56.1
2	Latham (29)	154	96	2:18:09.4
3	Paulhan	131	81	2:40:00.0
4	Lambert	116	72	1:50:59.2
5	Latham (13)	111	69	1:38:05.2
6	Tissandier	110	68	1:46:52.0

Gordon Bennett Cup

(2 Circuits, 10 Kilometers Each)

PLACE	PILOT	1ST CIRCUIT	2ND CIRCUIT	TIME
1	Curtiss	7:57.4	7:53.2	15:50.6
2	Blériot	7:53.2	8:03.0	15:56.2
3	Latham	8:51.0	8:41.0	17:32.0
4	Lefebvre	9:45.8	11:01.8	20:47.6

Prix de la Vitesse

(3 Circuits, 10 Kilometers Each)

PLACE	PILOT	TIME (MINS.)
1	Curtiss	23:29.0
2	Latham	24:18.2
3	Tissandier	28:59.2
4	Lefebvre	29:02.0

Prix de Tour de Piste

(1 Circuit, 10 Kilometers Each)

PLACE	PILOT	BEST TIME (MINS.)
1	Blériot	7:47.8
2	Curtiss	7:79.4

Prix des Passagers

(1 Circuit, 10 Kilometers Each)

PLACE	PILOT	NUMBER OF PASSENGERS	TIME (MINS.)
1	Farman	2	10:39.0
2	Farman	1	9:52.2
3	Lefebvre	1	10:39.0

Prix de l'Altitude

(1 Circuit, 10 Kilometers Each)

PLACE	PILOT	HEIGHTS REACHED	
		METERS	FEET
1	Latham	115	508
2	Farman	110	360

It was not until the final day of the meet that Hubert Latham gained the victory that had eluded him since his attempt to become the first to fly across the English Channel. He is shown here during the flight that won him the prestigious altitude prize, the Prix de l'Altitude.

Higher and higher Latham rose until his barograph read that he had reached a height of 508 feet—higher than anyone had ever gone. Amazingly, he had probably gone considerably higher. But at 508 feet, the barograph jammed and that was the figure that had to be officially recorded.

To many, Latham's landing was almost as extraordinary as his ascent. Returning to earth in a steep dive, he banked sharply when he got close to the ground and landed expertly behind the judges' enclosure. As soon as the Antoinette came to a halt, several women rushed

to the plane, jumped up onto Latham, and smothered him in kisses. Meantime, others in the grandstand tore down a section of the handrail so that they could personally greet Latham and help tow his plane to his hangar.

It was a spectacular ending to a spectacular week that had been more successful than even its greatest boosters could have imagined or hoped for. The more than one million people who witnessed the events represented one of the largest week-long gatherings of the era. The corporation that had organized the meet earned twenty times more money than it had invested in the endeavor, while the champagne manufacturers came away with twice as much in profits as they had donated in prizes. Along with the glory and the publicity they received, the pilots earned more than a million dollars in today's money in awards. And, judging by the extraordinary reactions of those who attended the meet ("Never since history began have there been witnessed such scenes of wonder," exclaimed the *New York Times*), the organizers had more than succeeded in delivering both the world's fair and the showcase of marvels they had set out to present.

But none of these were the most important result to come out of the air meet at Rheims. As one publication of the day stated, "Of the many thousands who went to [Rheims], not one left without feeling that he had seen history in the making." For, above all else, the Great Aviation Week at Rheims marked the beginning of an extraordinary era. As one visitor to the meet exclaimed, "I have seen the future and its name is flight."

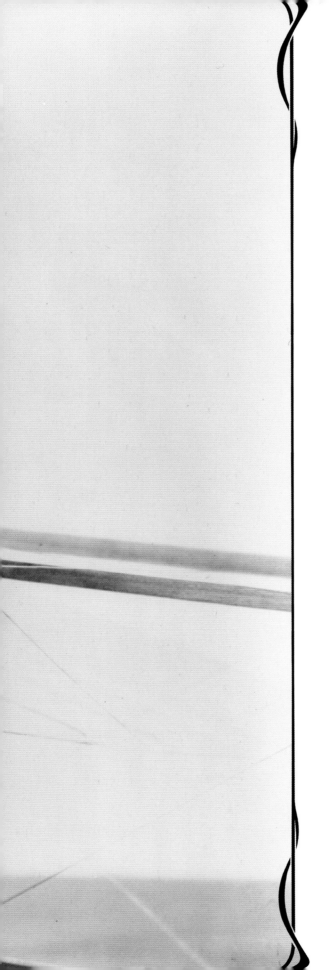

AVIATION TAKES FLIGHT:

A RHEIMS-INSPIRED DECADE

THANKS TO THE Grande Semaine de l'Aviation, a new era had begun. Glenn Curtiss's spellbinding race with Louis Blériot, Hubert Latham's amazing altitude record, and Henry Farman's astounding 116-mile flight had all shown that not only was aviation past its experimental stage, it was also looking more and more like the future. If any further proof was needed, the next ten years would yield achievements that the early visionaries of flight could only have dreamed of.

Women would play a major role in the growth of aviation. Pictured here is Harriet Quimby, one of the most celebrated of the early female aviators.

⌐ AIR SHOWS IN AMERICA ⌐

In the decade following Rheims, people's eyes increasingly turned to the skies. These onlookers were watching an air race at the 1910 Harvard-Boston Aero Meet.

IT BEGAN WITH THE AIR SHOWS that succeeded the grand week at Rheims. Given the triumph of that extravaganza, it was hardly surprising that it was immediately copied, and in 1910 three major meets took place in the United States alone. These Rheims-inspired gatherings attracted many of the world's leading aviators, drew enormous crowds that turned out to see their first real-life airplanes, and became the sites where records continued to be broken. And, as had happened at Rheims, each of these meets profoundly affected the future of American aviation

by inspiring such would-be pilots as Lincoln Beachey and Harriet Quimby.

The first of these meetings, the Los Angeles International Air Meet, took place January 10–20 at Dominguez Field in present-day Carson, California.

The meet, the first ever held in the United States, drew half a million people and was described by the *Los Angeles Times* as "one of the greatest public events in the history of the West." The great hero of the show was Louis Paulhan, who had brought two Farman biplanes and two Blériot monoplanes with him. Before the meet ended, Paulhan set a new altitude record of 4,164 feet, and also entertained the crowd by performing one of the first aerial bombing tests (using weights to simulate bombs). Glenn Curtiss also thrilled the spectators by setting a new speed record of 55 miles per hour and by winning the prize for the quickest takeoff.

The second great American air meet, and the first to be held in the East, was the Harvard-Boston Aero Meet, which was staged September 3–13, 1910. Among its attractions were performances by both the Wright brothers and the Glenn Curtiss exhibition teams. But it was the Englishman Claude Grahame-White who stole the show. The dashing young aviator not only won the $10,000 prize (about $260,000 in today's money) for best overall performance, but also won four individual events and finished second in three others.

Grahame-White was also the shining star of the third major American air meet staged in 1910, this one held at New York's Belmont Park racetrack October 22–31. The Englishman added to his growing reputation by winning the Gordon Bennett Cup with the flamboyant American pilot John Moisant finishing second.

WOMEN IN THE AIR

ALTHOUGH THERE WERE no female competitors at the Rheims air meet, by the end of the second decade of the 1900s women were making vital contributions in every area of aviation. Actually, there had been women in the air since the earliest days of flight. The first female to pilot a motorized aircraft was Aida de Acosta, an American vacationing in France, who, in June 1903, persuaded Alberto Santos-Dumont to permit her to pilot one of his dirigibles.

In 1910, Blanche Scott, flying for the newly established Glenn Curtiss Exhibition Company, became the first woman to take a solo heavier-than-air flight in the United States. Earlier, Scott had become the first woman to drive an automobile across the nation. Also in 1910, Raymonde de La Roche received the world's first official female pilot's license. Seven other French women quickly followed her, including Marie Marvingt, who was one of the first women to fly in combat when she carried out bombing raids over Germany during World War I.

By 1911 two female pilots in particular had gained great attention. One was Belgian champion bicyclist, motorcyclist, and automobile race driver Hélène Dutrieu, who, once she took up flying, became known as the "girl hawk" because of the extraordinary daring and skill she demonstrated in flight. The other was American magazine and movie writer Harriet Quimby, who, in 1911, became the first officially licensed woman pilot in the United States and who, in 1912, became the first woman to fly across the English Channel.

The first licensed African American female pilot was Bessie Coleman, who, because of racial discrimination, had to move to France to learn to fly.

At age sixteen, Elinor Smith became the youngest female to receive a pilot's license from the National Aeronautic Association. When she was seventeen, responding to a dare issued by a group of men who doubted her abilities, she flew underneath four bridges along New York City's East River.

Other female aviation stars of the period included Katherine Stinson, who, along with other flying achievements she attained, flew nonstop from San Diego to San Francisco in 1917, setting a nonstop long-distance record of 610 miles for both men and women. In the years following World War I, Ruth Law and Phoebe Fairgrave Omlie, two of the most daring and skilled of all the barnstorming pilots, would thrill the nation.

Bessie Coleman.

⟿ FROM LONDON TO MANCHESTER ⟿

LIKE THE PERIOD BEFORE IT, the decade following Rheims continued to witness advances in aviation that were the direct result of generous prizes offered by wealthy organizations or individuals.

One of the first of these had its roots in 1906 when the *Daily Mail* offered a prize of what would be more than $500,000 today to the first aviator to fly from London to Manchester, England, in less than 24 hours. No more than two landings along the way were allowed and the rules stipulated that the aviator had to start and finish within 5 miles of the *Daily Mail*'s London and Manchester offices. It was an enticing prize, but at the time it was offered it seemed totally unwinnable. The most accomplished aviator in Europe of 1906 was Alberto Santos-Dumont and he was only able to keep his plane aloft for a few seconds at a time. The popular magazine *Punch*, poking fun at what seemed to be an absurd contest, offered the same amount of money to the first pilot to fly to Mars and back in two weeks.

By 1910, however, as the Rheims meet had proved, so much progress had been made in airplanes and in flying ability that a two-stop, approximately 185-mile flight in less than 24 hours no longer seemed impossible, particularly to Claude Grahame-White and Louis Paulhan.

Both contenders were flying planes made by Henry Farman's manufacturing company and both were being personally coached by Farman. Grahame-White was the first to take off but after suffering engine problems he was forced to land near a town named Lichfield. While on the ground, the plane was blown over by high winds and suffered such extreme damage that Grahame-White was forced to have it hauled back to London for repairs.

Meantime, on April 27, 1910, Paulhan took off in pursuit of the prize. When, that evening, Grahame-White was told that Paulhan was headed for Manchester he made a bold and unprecedented move.

He made the first nighttime takeoff and flight in history. It was a brave attempt, but just as it seemed he might overtake Paulhan his engine gave out on him again and for the second time he was forced to make an emergency landing.

By this time the race had attracted enormous attention, with the New York *Evening Post* heralding it as "not the greatest of the century, but of all centuries." It may have been an overstatement but even though Paulhan was now approaching the finish line it was becoming increasingly dramatic. For the closer he got to Manchester, the stronger the winds became. So much so that, as he later wrote, "My machine rose viciously

"MY MACHINE ROSE VICIOUSLY AND THEN DROPPED SO QUICKLY."

and then dropped so quickly that I was almost torn from my seat. I had to hold onto the controls with all my strength. I climbed to more than [1,000 feet] in the hope of finding a calmer patch but the wind persisted."

Somehow, Paulhan hung on. And at 5:20 a.m., the large crowd awaiting the two pilots at a flying field just outside Manchester erupted in cheers as a speck of an airplane appeared in the distance. But which pilot was it? When the race had begun it had engendered great patriotic feelings—a sense of England versus France. But now that it was obviously producing a winner it didn't really matter As the London *Times* exclaimed, "No one cared then whether the aviator who approached was a Frenchman or Englishman. It was enough that he was a hero of the air." As it turned out, the great hero was Paulhan, victorious but shaken and freezing, vowing that he would never attempt a similar flight again. But in an age when such brave and daring souls would be remembered as "those magnificent men in their flying machines," it was a vow soon forgotten.

Following pages: Claude Grahame-White is credited with having made the first flight at night. Here a huge crowd mobs his plane during his race with Louis Paulhan from London to Manchester.

JOHN MOISANT

A NUMBER OF THE pioneer pilots who competed at Rheims, such as Glenn Curtiss and Louis Blériot, remain well-known today. Others, although important to the birth of aviation, have been lost to history. Among them is John Moisant. An airplane designer, flight instructor, businessman, political revolutionary, and a daring and fearless pilot, John Moisant was without question one of the most fascinating early fliers to take to the sky.

One of his sisters, Matilde, born in Kankakee, Illinois, in 1868, would become the second American woman to receive a pilot's license and would go on to break the women's world record for altitude. Moisant himself showed few early signs of being interested in flying, and in 1896 he and his three brothers, anxious to make their fortunes, moved to El Salvador and bought several sugarcane plantations.

The plantations proved highly successful and Moisant became wealthier than he could ever have imagined. But he also found himself caught up in the political turmoil that was so much a part of Central America at the time. In 1907, government troops swooped into one of the plantations, took two of Moisant's brothers off to jail, and charged them with being revolutionaries. These actions turned Moisant into a true rebel and, in 1907 and 1909, he led two failed rebellions and coup attempts against the El Salvadoran government.

Things then took a dramatic turn when the president of Nicaragua, impressed with Moisant's fiery spirit, asked him to go to France to investigate airplanes. It could not have been a more propitious time, for Moisant arrived in France just as the Great Aviation Week at Rheims was beginning. It took less than one day's attendance at the air meet for Moisant to fall completely in love with flying.

Between the conclusion of the Rheims meet and the spring of 1910, Moisant designed and built two airplanes. The first one was constructed entirely from aluminum and steel and thus became the first all-metal aircraft in the world. As soon as the two planes were completed, Moisant enrolled in Louis Blériot's flying school, where he received four lessons from the famous pilot himself. He then obtained his pilot's license and in a remarkably short period of time made an indelible mark on early aviation.

On August 9, 1910, he made two flights over Paris, each time carrying a passenger with him, one of them being the future legendary pilot Roland Garros. These were the first passenger flights ever made over a city. Eight days later, with his mechanic and his cat aboard, Moisant flew the first flight with a passenger across the English Channel.

Moisant's daring, crowd-pleasing flights at the Belmont air meet garnered him an enormous amount of publicity and soon after the meet ended, he, along with his brother, formed the Moisant International Aviators, one of the first shows called flying circuses that featured daredevil pilots and performed to large crowds throughout the United States.

He continued to fly competitively, though. On December 31, 1910, while making a test flight in the skies near New Orleans in preparation for the 1910 Michelin Cup, his plane was struck by turbulence, went into a nosedive, and crashed. The man who had earned the nickname King of the Aviators was thrown from his plane and killed.

↝ CROSSING THE ALPS ↝

FOR AVIATORS, the English Channel had been the first great geographical barrier to be overcome. But soon, another seemingly impregnable natural barrier captured the attention of pilots everywhere.

The Aero Club of Italy offered a cash prize of $20,000 (about $530,000 in today's money) to the first person able to fly through and above the Alps. Specifically, the contest called for participants to fly through the Simplon Pass in the Swiss Alps and then on to Milan, Italy, where an aviation meet was being held. It was an enormous challenge. To the west of the pass the mountains rose to 13,000 feet. The winds that high were often ferocious and could blow from any direction. And even though the rules of the contest allowed for the trip to Milan to be made in stages, the first leg through the mountains was twenty-five miles long with no possible landing.

Thirteen aviators officially entered the contest. The race committee, however, aware of the extreme danger and difficulties of the flight, accepted only the five who appeared to have the best chance of, if not winning the prize, at least surviving the attempt. Among them was a twenty-three-year-old aviator whose parents were Peruvian but who had been born in and lived in Paris. Given the birth name Jorge Antonio Chávez Dartnell, he was commonly called Jorge Chávez.

Chávez had received his pilot's license after attending the flying school established by Henry Farman and his brother. He had quickly proved himself to be an excellent pilot and by the time the contest got underway, he had set a new altitude world record of 8,840 feet.

In the fall of 1910, the competitors for the prize gathered on the Swiss side of the Simplon Pass at the town of Ried-Brig. What followed were several attempts by Chávez and his rivals to head for the pass, only to be forced back by heavy winds.

Finally, at 1:30 p.m. on September 23, 1910, after several days of being grounded because of the weather and failed attempts at reaching the pass by two of his competitors, Chávez took off again. More determined than ever, he told his supporters, "Whatever happens, I shall be found on the other side of the Alps."

This time he made it to the pass and flew through it. But as soon as he reached the Italian side, he encountered winds so violent they forced him to fly down a steep ravine where he hoped he would be able to avoid the worst of the turbulence. Surrounded by the towering black peaks and battling fiercely to keep the tiny wooden monoplane under control, he had never felt so alone. Several times his plane was blown within feet of the enormous rock faces. And more than once, as it hit especially strong air currents, his Blériot XI either rose or fell as much as 60 feet before

"WHATEVER HAPPENS, I SHALL BE FOUND ON THE OTHER SIDE OF THE ALPS."

he could bring it back under control. Yet, some 50 minutes after he had taken off, spectators waiting at the landing field at Domodossola on the Italian side of the pass spotted his plane and let out an enormous cheer. Chávez had done it. The impossible had been accomplished.

It certainly seemed so as Chávez glided toward a landing. But then, when he was little more than 30 feet from the ground, disaster struck. "I saw the two wings of the monoplane suddenly flatten out and paste themselves against the fuselage," one of the spectators stated. "Chávez was about a dozen meters up; he fell like a stone."

Severely injured, but still conscious, Chávez was taken to the hospital, where, after being declared the winner of the prize, he received congratulatory telegraphs from around the world. But he had lost an enormous amount of blood, and four days later he died. His final words, "higher, higher, higher," became an inspiration for generations of aviators who followed.

And only one year later a much longer and more difficult race would prove how far and how rapidly aviation had advanced since the heady days of the Rheims meet.

Once again it was motivated by a huge prize, this one offered by American newspaper tycoon William Randolph Hearst, who guaranteed that his newspaper chain would award $50,000 (about $1,300,000 in today's money) to the first pilot to fly across the United States in thirty days.

⌒ CROSSING THE UNITED STATES ⌒

IT WAS AN ENORMOUS PRIZE. But it was an even greater challenge, one that was eagerly accepted by one of the most daring of all the pioneer aviators, thirty-two-year-old Calbraith "Cal" Rodgers, the great-grandson of the legendary American naval hero Oliver Hazard Perry. As far as aviation had advanced, there were still no airports, no navigation maps, no control towers, no beacons to aid a pilot on even a short trip, let alone on an unheard-of nearly 2,700 miles across the nation. For guidance, Rodgers would have to follow railroad tracks and try to recognize landmarks.

STILL NO AIRPORTS, NO NAVIGATION MAPS, NO CONTROL TOWERS, NO BEACONS TO AID A PILOT.

Also, the flight would be expensive, and Rodgers would not be able to even attempt it without a sponsor. Fortunately, Armour, the giant meat-packaging company, knowing that the bold endeavor would attract enormous attention, saw the flight as a most effective way to advertise a new grape soft drink named Vin Fiz that it was launching. In return for putting the product's name on the rudder and under the wings of Rodgers's plane, Armour paid him a cash fee and provided him with a three-car train in which his support team could travel. The train carried two mechanics and their two assistants, Rodgers's wife and mother, fuel for the plane, repair parts to rebuild the aircraft, and spare engines. One of the three cars had a repair shop, and all three advertised Vin Fiz on their sides.

In what would become one of the most remarkable flights in the history of aviation, Rodgers took off from Sheepshead Bay, New York, late in the afternoon on September 17, 1911. Before his trip was over he crashed at least sixteen times and was forced to land more than fifty

A smiling Cal Rodgers sets the wheels of his completely rebuilt plane down on the shores of the Pacific Ocean after one of the most remarkable flights in history.

other times. The Vin Fiz plane was so badly damaged in the crashes that the entire craft had to be completely rebuilt at least twice. When his flight was finally over, all that remained of the original Vin Fiz plane was a rudder and a couple of wing struts. Rodgers himself was continually injured in the crashes, some of which resulted in his being hospitalized. But each time he recovered quickly and resumed his flight.

On November 5, 1911, forty-nine days after he had left Sheepshead Bay, Rodgers landed in Pasadena, California. Unfortunately, he had missed Hearst's deadline by nineteen days.

On November 12, determined to be able to claim that he had reached the Pacific Ocean, Rodgers took to the air again and headed for the ocean at Long Beach, California, some 20 miles away. Again, he encountered mechanical problems, and was forced down twice, the second time breaking an ankle. Still unwilling to give up, he took off again on December 10, 1911, and this time put down on the beach and taxied into the Pacific Ocean. He had flown 4,000 miles, farther than any pilot had ever flown.

⟿ CROSSING THE MEDITERRANEAN ⟿

ONE OF THE LEGIONS of who had been inspired by these bold achievements was Roland Garros. He was an aviator who, before he too would die much too young, became one of the world's most honored fliers. On September 23, 1913, Garros took off from the Fréjus airdrome in the south of France and headed for Tunisia on the African coast in a daring attempt to become the first to overcome yet another danger-fraught natural obstacle: flying across the Mediterranean Sea.

Problems with the weather, particularly the wind, had plagued Garros's attempt even before he took off. When these problems continued once he was in the air, he decided that even though it would increase the duration of his attempt, and use up more fuel, it would be wise to change the course of his flight. His original plan was to fly a straight path along the coasts of the Mediterranean islands of Corsica and Sardinia. But because he was worried about fuel consumption, and because his engine was not performing perfectly, he decided to fly directly over the two islands in case he had to make an emergency landing.

Flying on, he passed over Corsica without incident and headed for Sardinia. He was almost directly over that island's capital, Cagliari, when suddenly the wind increased dramatically, and his engine began to sputter and give signs of quitting. It was a dire situation, one that threatened to end in disaster. "I was lost in the clouds," Garros would later write, "around 9842 feet and I had no way of knowing if the plane was moving forwards or backwards, if I was diverted from the flight path on the right or on the left because of the wind. . . . I could say, without exaggerating, that as a pilot, I have never experienced such a difficult hour or flight in my career."

"AS A PILOT, I HAVE NEVER EXPERIENCED SUCH A DIFFICULT HOUR OR FLIGHT IN MY CAREER."

Certain that his engine was going to die and that he was about to plunge into the sea, Garros tried desperately to find a break in the clouds so he could search the horizon for the African coast. Finally, finding a break, he peered down at the sea. Before he had taken off, the French government had offered to send a cruiser to accompany him on his route. He had refused but French naval officers had nonetheless sent their torpedo boats out to await his arrival. Spotting the vessels, Garros dove down toward them. Ten minutes later, after following them, he spotted the coast of Tunisia.

At 1:45 p.m. he landed in the Tunisian community of Bizerte, the northernmost city in Africa. He had been in the air just 7 minutes shy of 8 hours and had traveled 500 miles. When mechanics checked his fuel tank they found that it was completely empty.

A REMARKABLE PLANE

OF ALL THE FLIGHTS that took place in the decade following the Rheims air meet, one of the most spectacular of all was that taken in June 1914 by Russian pilot and aircraft designer Igor Sikorsky. A year earlier, Sikorsky had designed one of the largest planes of the day, a 4-engine airplane with a wingspan of more than 113 feet.

The plane shocked Sikorsky's detractors, but he had a bigger surprise for them. In October 1913, he built an even larger plane. Called the Ilya Muromets, it had 4 giant 100-horsepower engines, a wingspan of over 105 feet, and a fuselage more than 77 feet long. When fully loaded,

THE AIRCRAFT HAD A BALCONY THAT OFFERED PASSENGERS SPECTACULAR VIEWS.

it weighed over 12,000 pounds. Built to carry 16 people, including the crew, the plane featured such innovations as a heated passenger cabin that also had electric lights, a bedroom, and the first toilet ever installed in an airplane. At its front the aircraft had a balcony that offered passengers spectacular views. On its rear fuselage, it had an open observation platform intended to provide the most daring passengers with an even more thrilling aerial experience.

On June 30, 1914, Sikorsky and a three-man crew departed in the Ilya Muromets on an unprecedented aerial journey to the Russian city of Kiev. It was to be a 1,600-mile round-trip flight over forest, swamps, and other wilderness, all without the accompanying guidance of trains or motorcars or ships.

The first leg of the trip proved uneventful. But soon after landing and taking off from a refueling site at Orsha, one of the plane's engines caught fire, forcing two of the crew members to climb onto the wing and beat out the flames with their coats. After making an emergency landing stop for repairs, the Ilya Muromets continued on, only to encounter wind, rain, and turbulence so strong that at one point the plane was thrown into a spin and plunged 1,000 feet before Sikorsky could bring the mammoth plane back under control.

Fortunately, the landing at Kiev and the trip back to St. Petersburg were uneventful and, after what had been a 26-hour flight, Sikorsky returned to a hero's welcome. When World War I began, the Ilya Muromets was converted by Russia, which fought on the side of the Allies, into a bomber and proved to be one of the most effective military weapons of the war.

☞ AIRPLANES AT WAR ☜

BY 1914, IT SEEMED as if the steady progression of triumphs in the air would never end. Then suddenly something happened that few had foreseen: The world went to war. The eruption of World War I brought a dramatic halt to air meets and races, the conquering of natural barriers, and the pursuit of altitude and speed records. One of the biggest questions that emerged was: What role, if any, would the airplane play in the conflict?

There was no shortage of people, including many in high places, who shared the opinion of the British war secretary, who stated, "We do not consider that aeroplanes will be of any possible use for war purposes." Others, including the Wright brothers, took a totally opposite view, with Orville writing sadly toward the end of the bloody conflict, "When my brother and I built and flew the first man-carrying flying machine, we thought we were introducing into the world an invention

BARNSTORMERS

OUT OF WORLD WAR I came a group of men and women who helped popularize flying more than ever by introducing millions of people in the nation's rural areas to the airplane. These aviators were called "barnstormers" and they were the daredevils of their day. Traveling from town to town and performing almost any stunt with an airplane that anyone could imagine, they put on shows and breathtaking demonstrations that became one of post–World War I America's most popular forms of entertainment.

There were two main factors that led to the growth of barnstorming. One was the number of former World War I aviators who, more than anything else, now wanted to make a living by flying. The other was the huge number of a special type of plane left over from the war. This plane was called a Jenny. It was built by Glenn Curtiss's company and had been used to train American military pilots. Now the government was practically giving them away and many of them were bought by fliers who used them to go barnstorming.

In most rural towns, the appearance of a barnstorming group would lead to what was akin to a national holiday. Schools and businesses shut down so that people could hustle out to the farm (thus the name barnstormer) where the show was taking place and watch the performances and, thrill of all thrills, even purchase a ride on an airplane.

Among the dozens of antics designed to terrify and delight spectators were wing-walking, upside-down flying, transferring between airplanes—when an aviator switched from one plane to another during a flight—and even playing tennis on the wings of flying aircraft. Perhaps the most extreme was a "dive of death." This stunt required the pilot to dive straight down until perilously close to the ground and then pull back up at the very last moment.

Although most barnstormers performed on their own or in small groups, one of the most popular attractions were what was known as "flying circuses." Made up of several planes and pilots, some traveled to every state in the nation and a number performed overseas. Among the most popular was the Gates Flying Circus, which became known not only for its stunts but also for initiating the one-dollar joyride. These rides became so popular that in a single day in a show in Steubenville, Ohio, one of Gates's pilots took 980 passengers up for rides.

"Jersey" Ringel.

Yet barnstorming was all over by 1927, its demise brought about by the number of restrictions placed on the barnstormers and their planes due to the government's concern over the increasingly large number of fatalities that were resulting from the "death-defying" acts that were being performed.

It had, however, been a unique, exciting, and important time. Among the barnstormers was Charles Lindbergh, who not only learned to fly on the barnstorming circuit but also performed such stunts as wingwalking and trick parachuting. Bessie Coleman was another flying pioneer with barnstorming roots.

which would make further wars practically impossible." The truth of the matter was that as the war began no one really knew how the airplane would be used in the conflict.

During the first months of the fighting, the airplane's role was confined solely to reconnaissance, specifically that of detecting and photographing enemy positions. Almost none of the observation aircraft carried weapons. If two enemy reconnaissance planes met in the air, the pilots were likely to give a friendly wave to each other and go on about their business.

That all changed when, thanks primarily to Roland Garros and Anthony Fokker, a system of safely firing a machine gun straight ahead through the revolving blades of a plane's propeller was developed. The birth of the fighter plane confirmed the words of an Italian military officer who predicted, "The sky is about to become another battlefield no less important than the battlefields on land and sea." By the end of the war, each nation had its own leading fighter pilots, called "aces." The most famous ace of the war was the man who became known as the Red Baron, Germany's Baron Manfred von Richthofen, who shot down eighty Allied planes.

The often-spectacular one-on-one air battles, known as dogfights, that took place during the conflict provided some of the most dramatic moments of World War I. And the hundreds of Allied bombers that pounded German troops, railroad junctions, and supply depots in the final weeks of the war hastened the conflict's end. But it was the way in which the war placed more demands on airplanes than ever before that had the greatest effect on the future of aviation. World War I marked the first time that airplanes were operated on a daily basis, leading to the

BY THE END OF THE WAR, EACH NATION HAD ITS OWN LEADING FIGHTER PILOTS, CALLED "ACES."

Facing page: In the early days of World War I, the airplane was used almost exclusively to spot the movements of the various troops. By the conflict's end, airplanes would become far more lethal weapons.

John Alcock and Arthur Brown take off from Newfoundland headed for Ireland. Almost sixteen hours later they shocked the world by becoming the first to fly nonstop across the Atlantic.

need for and the creation of much improved means of repairing them and keeping them in top flying condition. And, as all the warring nations demanded sturdier planes and mightier engines, aircraft became faster, stronger, and more powerful. There was also a dramatic change in the number of airplanes built. Before the war, planes had been manufactured in the hundreds; now they were produced in the thousands.

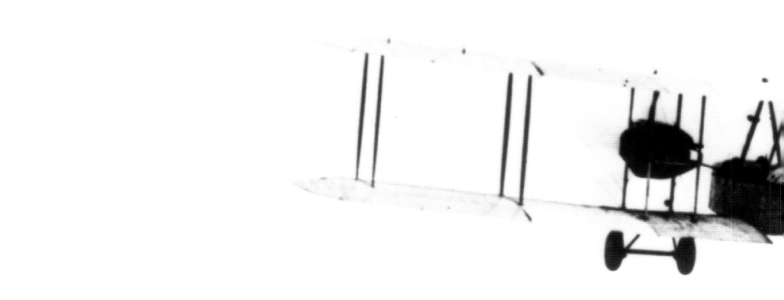

CROSSING THE ATLANTIC

By 1919, a full decade after Rheims, the promise of what the airplane held in store, first fully revealed at what had already become regarded as a legendary gathering, was being fulfilled. But the greatest test of the airplane's prowess still remained. It was the Atlantic Ocean that Winston Churchill, who in 1919 was England's secretary of state for war and air,

called "a terrible waste of desolate waters, tossing in tumult in repeated and almost ceaseless storms, and shrouded with an unbroken canopy of mist."

This was true, but the Atlantic was also the most valuable commercial and military avenue in the world. But could it be flown? As Churchill also stated, the aviators who tried to do it would be threatened every long mile of the way with "destruction from a drop of water in the carburetor, or a spot of oil on their plugs, or a tiny gram of dirt in the feed pipe, or from any of the other hundred and one indirect causes [which] might drop an aeroplane to its fate."

It certainly seemed an impossible challenge. But when the *Daily Mail* offered what in today's money would be a $500,000 prize for the first person or persons to fly nonstop across the Atlantic, four two-man teams emerged as serious contenders.

Among them were two men, John Alcock and Arthur Brown, who had much in common. Both Alcock, as a pilot, and Brown, as a navigator, were obsessed with flying. Both had served in the Royal (British) Air Force during World War I. Both aviators had been shot down and captured and both had spent their time in prison camp thinking of ways the Atlantic might be crossed nonstop by air.

By the spring of 1919, Alcock and Brown and their plane, a converted World War I bomber called a Vickers Vimy, had arrived in Newfoundland, off the east coast of Canada, the most advantageous spot in America from which to attempt a nonstop flight to Europe. The three other contending teams were there also, but by June 14 one of them had crashed on takeoff, another had crashed in the Atlantic, and the third gave indication that it would probably abandon any attempt. On June 14, 1919, Alcock and Brown took to the sky.

It was the most harrowing flight imaginable. Flying in an open cockpit with the wind continually pounding against them, they immediately encountered dense fog that stayed with them for almost their entire flight. Only a few miles out, their radio went dead and they lost all communication with anyone. Almost as soon as that happened, they flew directly into the most vicious storm that either man had ever encountered. Turbulence tugged the Vimy around like a toy. Then true disaster struck. The Vimy stalled out completely and went into a deep dive, heading directly for the Atlantic. It was not until they were less than 10 feet from the ocean that, miraculously, Alcock was able to pull the plane out of the stall and avert certain death.

Their challenges were far from over, though. As temperatures dropped, snow and ice appeared and began clogging the air intakes of the Vimy's two engines. Five times, Brown had to climb out onto the wing to chip away the ice before the engines stalled while Alcock fought desperately to keep the plane on an even keel.

> ## TURBULENCE TUGGED THE VIMY AROUND LIKE A TOY. THEN TRUE DISASTER STRUCK. THE VIMY STALLED OUT COMPLETELY AND WENT INTO A DEEP DIVE.

In the midmorning of June 15, as if to reward the two men for all they had overcome, the skies cleared for the first time and they spotted the coast of Ireland. Although they mistook a water-filled bog for a smooth green field and landed nose down, tail up, in a ditch, they had done it. In flying 1,890 miles, the farthest anyone had ever flown, in 16 hours and 12 minutes, they had become the first to conquer the Atlantic in a nonstop flight.

Around the world, Alcock and Brown were hailed as the heroes they truly were. Back in America, a seventeen-year-old boy told his friends that the flight had inspired him to put all his efforts into accomplishing something similar. His name was Charles Lindbergh.

POSTSCRIPT:
WHAT HAPPENED TO THE PILOTS?

LOUIS BLÉRIOT

Although the crash that Blériot suffered on the last day of the meet at Rheims convinced him that it was time to stop flying competitively, he did honor commitments he had made to take part in at least four other airshows in Europe. On December 10, 1910, however, flying under extremely windy conditions in Istanbul, Turkey, he crashed on top of a house, breaking several ribs and suffering internal injuries. Hospitalized for three weeks, he knew it was time to end his flying career.

Now concentrating on his airplane manufacturing company, Blériot, between 1910 and the beginning of World War I in 1914, built more than nine hundred planes, making him, along with the Voisin brothers and the Farman brothers, one of the largest airplane manufacturers in Europe.

In 1913, a consortium led by Blériot bought the French aircraft maker Société pour les Appareils Deperdussin. Blériot renamed it Société pour l'Aviation et Ses Dérives (SPAD) and under his direction this company produced some of the most effective fighter aircraft of World War I, particularly the SPAD S.XIII.

In 1927, having long been retired from flying, Blériot was on hand to welcome Charles Lindbergh when he landed in Paris at the completion of his nonstop flight across the Atlantic. Separated in age by thirty years, the two aviators were nonetheless forever linked by having been the first to fly across two famous bodies of water.

Blériot remained in the airplane-manufacturing business until his death in Paris on August 2, 1936. After a funeral with full military honors, he was buried at Versailles.

LOUIS-CHARLES BRÉGUET

Louis-Charles Bréguet, the pilot who experienced one of the most spectacular crashes at Rheims, went on to enjoy one of the longest and most successful lives of all the pioneer aviators. Bréguet was passionately interested in air transportation and in 1911 an airplane constructed by his company became the first to carry twelve passengers aloft.

During World War I, Bréguet's company grew enormously as it produced some 8,000 of what became the famous Bréguet XIV reconnaissance planes for the Allied Forces. During the years immediately following the conflict, the greatly advanced Bréguet XIX made aviation history by its ability to fly long distances over continents and oceans.

Bréguet's airplane-manufacturing company continued to lead the French aviation industry in the production of civil and military aircraft, and in 1919 he established a new commercial airline company called Compagnie des Messageries Avienne, which is now a world leader under the name Air France.

Over the years, Bréguet's airplanes continually set important records. In 1917, one of his planes made the first nonstop crossing of the south Atlantic. In 1933, another made a

4,500-mile flight across the Atlantic Ocean, the longest nonstop Atlantic flight up to that time.

Bréguet also became a pioneer in the development of the helicopter-like aircraft called a "gyroplane." In 1935, one of his gyroplanes, also called an autogiro, set a speed record of 61 miles per hour. The next year it established an altitude record of 517 feet.

One of the most respected men in the aviation industry, Bréguet, who won many honors for his contributions, remained active until he died in 1955 at Saint Germain-en-Laye, France, at the age of seventy-five.

ÉTIENNE BUNAU-VARILLA

Bunau-Varilla, the youngest pilot to compete in the 1904 Rheims air meet, also took part in the Rheims meet of 1910. Shortly afterward he turned to bicycle racing and, in partnership with another man, designed a streamlined, enclosed bicycle that beat the world record for speed.

Bunau-Varilla was drawn back to flying when World War I began, and he joined the French air force. On May 17, 1915, he was the first World War I pilot to become a prisoner of war when engine trouble forced him to land the plane in which he and a French general were flying inside German territory. Eventually the general managed to escape, but Bunau-Varilla spent two years in a prison camp.

After the war, he took up skiing and became captain of the French national ski team. Thanks to his enormously wealthy father, he spent the rest of his days at ski resorts and attending motorcar races, unabashedly boasting that he had never worked a day in his life. He died on December 12, 1961.

GEORGE COCKBURN

COCKBURN, THE SOLE BRITISH AVIATOR to compete at the Rheims air meet, devoted much of his life after the meet to training pilots for both the English army and navy. He also became a leading advocate for safety in flying. In 1912, he helped found the Royal Aero Club's Public Safety and Accidents Investigation Committee.

With the outbreak of World War I in 1914, Cockburn became an airplane inspector for the Royal Flying Corps. He served with such distinction that when the conflict ended, he received one of Great Britain's highest awards, an OBE (the Most Excellent Order of the British Empire). Cockburn died in England in 1931 at the age of fifty-nine.

GLENN CURTISS

AFTER RHEIMS, Glenn Curtiss competed in several other air meets and races while, at the same time, continuing to grow his airplane-manufacturing company into one of the largest in the world. Of all the post-Rheims flights he took, none was more important than the one he completed in May 1910, in response to a $10,000 prize (about $258,000 in today's money) offered by publisher Joseph Pulitzer. The prize was to be awarded to the first person to make the first long-distance flight between two major cities in the United States, specifically, a 150-mile flight from Albany to New York City.

On May 29, 1910, Curtiss, following the Hudson River and flying in an airplane he had named the *Hudson Flyer*, claimed the prize by completing the historic trip in just under four hours.

Also in 1910, Curtiss made several other contributions to the further development of aviation. In June he gave a simulated bombing demonstration to high-ranking American naval officers. In September he trained Blanche Stuart Scott, widely regarded as the first woman aviator in America. And on November 10, 1910, Eugene Ely, a member of Curtiss's demonstration team, achieved the first-ever takeoff from the deck of a ship, setting the stage for the development of the vessel that would change naval history: the aircraft carrier.

In July 1911, Curtiss sold the U.S. Navy their first aircraft, a seaplane named the A-1 Triad. The A-1 was also equipped with retractable wheels, making it the world's first amphibian plane. It was the beginning of a relationship between Curtiss and the U.S. Navy that would ultimately lead to his becoming known as the "Father of Naval Aviation."

In 1914, on the eve of World War I, Curtiss designed a two-engine flying boat named the *America*. Eventually the Curtiss factory built sixty-eight "Large Americas," which, under the name H-12, became the only American-designed and American-built aircraft that saw combat in World War I.

In 1916, as it became clear that America would become involved in the conflict, the U.S. Army asked Curtiss to develop a simple, easy-to-fly and maintain, two-seat airplane that it could use to train its pilots. In response, Curtiss designed what became one of the most famous planes in aviation history—the JN-4, nicknamed the "Jenny." Before the war was over, Curtiss, at the request of the navy, would also design another aircraft destined for fame. It was the 4-engine flying boat known as the NC-4, which in 1919, would become the first airplane to cross the Atlantic Ocean (although not nonstop).

For the Curtiss Aeroplane and Motor Company, the end of World War I brought a downturn in military contracts, and Curtiss found himself spending an increased amount of time involved in his old love: participating in airplane races. Then, in 1921, to the surprise of many of his colleagues, he abruptly left the aviation world and became involved in land development, where he became as successful as he had been in flying and aircraft design and production. By 1930 he had, with friends, developed the Florida cities of Hialeah, Miami Springs, and Opa-locka.

While undergoing what was supposedly routine surgery for appendicitis in Buffalo, New York, Curtiss developed a blood clot and died; he was fifty-two years old. In honor of his amazing career, the aviator was inducted into the National Aviation Hall of Fame in 1964, the Motorsports Hall of Fame of America in 1990, and the Motorcycle Hall of Fame in 1998.

LÉON DELAGRANGE

ONE MONTH AFTER COMPETING at the Rheims air meet, Léon Delagrange set a world record for speed, at the Doncaster (England) Aviation Meeting by flying a Blériot monoplane 6 miles in 7 minutes and 36 seconds for an average of 50 miles an hour. Adding to the feat was the fact that Delagrange accomplished it while flying through a major storm.

The achievement became front-page news throughout the nation, but less than ten weeks later Delagrange made headlines again; this time on a tragic note. On January 4, 1910, in Bordeaux, France, while attempting to break Henry Farman's distance/endurance record, he was killed when his plane plunged 65 feet to the ground after both its wings had collapsed. Obituaries around the globe emphasized that Delagrange was one of the first in the world to have taken part in the adventure of flying.

HENRY FARMAN

On November 4, 1909, less than three months after he had been the most successful pilot at the Rheims air meet, Henry Farman added to his reputation as the world's greatest long-distance flier. At a meet at Mourmelon, France, he shattered the distance/duration record he had set at Rheims by achieving a flight of over 144 miles in 4 hours, 17 minutes, and 53 seconds.

Farman would continue to fly in selected events, but for the next thirty years he would devote most of his attention to the Farman Aviation Works, the airplane manufacturing company he had founded in 1907 with his two brothers, Richard and Maurice. From the beginning, the company was highly successful, and Farman airplanes took their place alongside Blériots, Voisins, and Wrights as the most popular of all the early aircraft.

During its thirty-year history, the Farman Aviation Works designed and built more than two hundred types of aircraft. Throughout World War I, its 1914 model was used arguably more than any other plane for reconnaissance, including artillery observation and troop movement. Included among the other important aircraft that Henry Farman and his brothers gave to the world was a plane called Goliath, the first long-distance passenger airliner, which began regular Paris-to-London flights on February 8, 1919.

The Farman Aviation Works was still going strong in 1937, having, for several years, added the production of cars and boats to its product line. That year, the French government announced it was nationalizing the aviation industry, meaning the government was taking over the design and construction of all aircraft. With the news, Henry Farman retired. He died in Paris on July 18, 1958.

HUBERT LATHAM

ALMOST FROM THE MOMENT the Rheims air meet ended, Latham began participating in other aerial competitions. Between late 1910 and early 1911, he appeared in twelve air meets, eight in Europe and four in the United States. On January 7, 1910, in Mourmelon, France, he set a new altitude record of 3,600 feet. Three months later, he established a new air speed record of 48.146 miles per hour. And in July 1910, during the second Rheims air meet, he broke his own altitude mark by climbing to 4,451 feet.

Later in 1910, while competing in the United States, Latham experienced two unique achievements. In November, during an air show in Baltimore, he participated in a simulated bomb-dropping exercise. Using sacks of flour instead of bombs, the aviator thrilled the crowds and the military officials in attendance by dropping one directly down the funnel of a battleship. In December, while taking part in a meet in Los Angeles, the flier was invited by a wealthy private citizen to come to his estate and try to shoot wild ducks from his airplane. Latham agreed to do so. After borrowing a shotgun, he shot down two of the fowl, thus becoming the first person known to have hunted wildlife from an aircraft.

For a man who had gained such widespread popularity not only for his flying skills, but also because of his open, flamboyant personality, it was ironic that Latham's life ended shrouded in mystery. Late in December 1911, he traveled to the French Congo on what remains an unknown mission. What is known is his body was found June 1912. Although Latham was an experienced and proficient hunter, the official report of his death stated that he was killed by a wounded buffalo. However, the adjutant-commander of the French Colonial Army who had discovered Latham's body swore that there were no marks on the aviator's body consistent with a wild animal attack. Later, conflicting testimony by porters who had been with Latham indicated that he may well have been killed by other porters in an attempt to steal his rifles. To this day, no one knows for certain what really happened to the man about whom early aviation expert Harry Harper said, "I do not think there was ever a finer pilot."

EUGÈNE LEFEBVRE

ONLY NINE DAYS after having been one of the stars of the Rheims meet, Lefebvre was killed while testing an airplane over Juvisy, France, when the aircraft suddenly plunged to the ground. In suffering this fate, Lefebvre became the first person to die while piloting a powered airplane and the second to be killed in an airplane crash.

LÉON LEVAVASSEUR

THREE MONTHS AFTER the Rheims air meet, Léon Levavasseur left the Antoinette Company, but he returned as its technical director in March 1910. Once back at the company he had founded, he designed the Antoinette military monoplane, which became known as the Monobloc. With its streamlined fuselage and cantilever wings, Levavasseur had high hopes for the plane. But during military trials held at Rheims in 1911, the Monobloc, because of its huge weight and underpowered engine, failed in every attempt it made to take off and was rejected by the military. The Antoinette Company went bankrupt shortly after.

Levavasseur made a comeback in 1918 through his design of an airplane with a set of wings that could be swept back and then returned to normal position for greater maneuverability. He won a "Safety in Aeroplanes" award for this innovation, but his financial situation failed to improve. In early 1922, the man who had contributed so much to the development of controlled, powered, heavier-than-air flight died in poverty.

LORD NORTHCLIFFE

BY THE OUTBREAK of World War I, Lord Northcliffe had become the most powerful newspaper owner in the world. Once the war began, Northcliffe also played an important role. In 1917, he directed a mission to the United States that in many ways bolstered America's full participation in the fight. A year later, he became director of enemy propaganda, in charge of, among other things, spreading news of German atrocities around the world.

Northcliffe was so effective at producing anti-German propaganda that a German warship was sent to shell his house, on the English coast, in an attempt to kill him. The house still bears a shell hole, kept in honor of Northcliffe's gardener's wife, who was killed in the attack.

Northcliffe's own life did not have a good ending. He became increasingly paranoid and irrational, issuing orders to his staff that made absolutely no sense. He died from heart disease in a hut on the roof of his house in London in August 1922.

LOUIS PAULHAN

AFTER SETTING A WORLD RECORD for altitude at the Los Angeles air meet of 1910 and winning the historic London-to-Manchester air race in 1911, Paulhan became a seaplane pioneer and designed and constructed a number of aircraft, including several for Glenn Curtiss's seaplane company. In 1913 he was hired by the Serbian government to develop aviation in that country.

During World War I, Paulhan flew combat missions in Serbia, and he also worked as a test pilot. When the war ended, he returned to designing seaplanes and continued to test fly planes. In 1937, one of flight's most important pioneers abruptly retired from aviation when his test pilot son was killed in an accident. Paulhan himself died on February 10, 1963.

HENRI ROUGIER

OF ALL THOSE who took part in the world's first international air meet, Henri Rougier had arguably the busiest post-Rheims life of them all. In September 1909, in the first air meet after Rheims, Rougier beat Glenn Curtiss for the altitude prize. Later that month he won the prizes for both distance and altitude at the Grand Prix of Berlin. Before the year was out, he competed in air meetings at Frankfurt, Germany; Blackpool, England, where he finished second overall; and Antwerp, Belgium, where he won all the races that were held.

In 1910, Rougier became a partner in an airplane-manufacturing company and spent considerable time personally demonstrating the finished products throughout Europe. In January 1911, Rougier returned to one of his first great loves when he entered and won a major new automobile race, the Monte-Carlo Rally. Shortly afterward he became the Paris agent and chief publicist for two automobile manufacturers, posts he held until the outbreak of World War I.

When the war was over, Rougier manufactured a select number of Rougier motorcars and also owned and operated a successful agency that sold highly popular Turcat-Méry automobiles. Returning to car racing, in 1923, he competed in both the French and Italian Grand Prix races.

Rougier lived out his retirement years in the small village of Toulou, France, and died in 1956 in Marseilles at the age of eighty.

ALBERTO SANTOS-DUMONT

UNFORTUNATELY FOR THE MAN who many, to this day, believe was really the first to fly a powered, controlled airplane, the final decades of his life were terribly unkind. Alberto Santos-Dumont's last flight as a pilot took place on January 4, 1910, and ended unhappily when a wing on his Demoiselle collapsed, causing the plane to crash. Fortunately, Santos-Dumont suffered only bruises, but two months later he announced his retirement from aviation. In June 1910, in an extraordinarily magnanimous gesture, Santos-Dumont allowed magazines around the world to freely publish detailed drawings of the aircraft so that people with limited resources could afford to build their own planes. "This machine," stated *Popular*

Mechanics, which printed the drawings in the United States, "is better than any other which has ever been built, for those who wish to reach results with the least possible expense."

In 1911, Santos-Dumont moved to a French seaside village, and he took up astronomy as a hobby. Three years later, with World War I underway, French police acted on an unsubstantiated tip and broke into his home and searched it. They thought he was spying on French naval movements. Terribly upset by the false allegations and deeply depressed by the fact that he had been diagnosed with multiple sclerosis, Santos-Dumont reacted by burning all his reports, reminiscences, and aeronautical plans and charts. He spent a number of years in sanatoriums grappling with his illness.

Santos-Dumont returned to Brazil in 1928. The man who had been instrumental in the development of every aspect of early flight had become more depressed than ever, particularly about his illness and his despair over the way airplanes were increasingly being developed as weapons of war. On July 23, 1932, Alberto Santos-Dumont took his own life. He was fifty-nine years old.

ROGER SOMMER

FOLLOWING RHEIMS, Roger Sommer participated in two other air meets—at Spa in Belgium, and at Doncaster in England. Then, having decided to make a career change, he sold his airplane and began designing and building aircraft.

Several of his early planes were successful during the 1910 air meets, and by the end of the year his company had orders for over sixty planes. In March 1911, one of the several different types of biplanes he designed and built carried twelve passengers. Shortly afterward, his aviation company designed and built a monoplane that won several races and prizes in meetings across Europe in both 1911 and 1912.

In 1913, due in great measure to the death of two of his key employees in accidents, Sommer closed his company, which by this time had produced 182 planes and 36 pilots who had qualified for their licenses at the company's flying schools. Sommer then joined his family's cloth-making business and helped turn it into one of the most diversified and successful companies in Europe. Sommer passed away on April 14, 1965, in Sainte-Maxime, France, at the age of eighty-seven.

PAUL TISSANDIER

TISSANDIER, WHO BEFORE BECOMING an airplane pilot and competing at Rheims, had been first a hot-air balloonist and then an airship pilot, spent

all but ten years of the rest of his life as an officer of the Fédération Aéronautique Internationale, an organization dedicated to the advancement of aviation throughout the world. Tissandier was the federation's treasurer from its founding in 1919 until 1923, and he served as its secretary-general until his death in 1945.

In 1952, in honor of the many contributions that Tissandier made to aviation, the Fédération Aéronautique Internationale established the Paul Tissandier Diploma, which has become one of the most prestigious awards in the field of flight. Winners have included some of the most accomplished and innovative individuals from every area of aviation.

GABRIEL VOISIN

His airplane-manufacturing company more successful than ever after his planes had received so much exposure at the 1910 Rheims air meet,

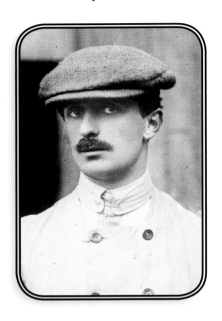

Gabriel Voisin developed a brand-new aircraft, the Canard Voisin. Radically designed, with its main wings placed at the rear of the plane, the Canard Voisin became highly popular for the next thirty years. When Voisin added floats to the airplane, it became the first seaplane in the French navy.

After World War I ended, Voisin underwent a major life change. He was deeply affected by the death and destruction caused by his airplane the Voisin III, one of the most effective aircrafts of the war. Shocking the flying world by completely abandoning aviation, he turned to manufacturing luxury automobiles, some of which became among the most highly valued motorcars in the world.

In 1945, Voisin underwent another dramatic change when he switched from manufacturing luxury automobiles to producing a car for the masses called a Biscooter. For the next ten years, the small, basic vehicle was highly popular throughout Europe, particularly in Spain.

In 1960, Voisin retired to his country home near Tournus, France, where he spent his remaining years writing his memoirs. He died at ninety-three in Ozenay, located in the Burgundy region of France.

WILBUR AND ORVILLE WRIGHT

After Wilbur, Orville, and Katharine Wright returned home from Europe, they were invited to the White House by President William Howard Taft, who, on behalf of a grateful nation, thanked them for all they had achieved. Dayton, Ohio, followed this tribute with a two-day celebration in honor of their hometown heroes.

It did not take long for a Wright brother to make headlines again. On October 4, 1909, as a feature of New York City's Hudson-Fulton Celebration, Wilbur, after lashing a canoe to the bottom of his plane in case of an emergency water landing, made a 33-minute, 20-mile flight around the Statue of Liberty and up and down the Hudson River. More than one million people turned out to view the flight.

In late May 1910, the brothers returned to Huffman Prairie, where on May 25, Orville piloted two very special flights. First, he took a 6-minute flight with Wilbur as his passenger. It was a unique aerial journey. Early on, they had promised their father that to avoid a double tragedy they would never fly together. Thus, this 6-minute trip was the only time the Wright brothers ever shared a flight. On the same day, another first was achieved. The brothers' father, Milton, had never flown in an airplane. Once Orville landed with Wilbur, he took his father on a 7-minute flight, the only one of the elder Wright's life.

In May 1911, another milestone in the Wright brothers' lives took place. Wilbur went back to Europe, where, in Berlin, he gave a flying lesson to a German pilot. It was the last time Wilbur would ever fly in an airplane. Orville, on the other hand, was not through setting records. Accompanied by one of his other brothers, Lorin, one of his nephews, and a friend, he returned to Kitty Hawk to conduct further flying experiments with gliders. There, on October 24, 1911, he set a world unpowered-flight soaring record of 9 minutes and 45 seconds.

Some six months later, tragedy struck, though. Wilbur fell sick with an illness that was eventually identified as typhoid fever. On May 30, 1912, despite a gallant battle against the disease, he passed away. Wilbur Wright was forty-five years old.

By this time, the Wright Company, of which Wilbur had been president and Orville vice president, was more successful than ever, with its headquarters in New York, a factory in Dayton, and a flying school at Huffman Prairie. For four years after Wilbur's death, Orville ran the company, but in 1916 he sold it, and built himself an aeronautics labora-tory so that he could pursue his first love—inventing. He also spent much of his remaining years serving on aeronautical boards and committees, including the National Advisory Committee for Aeronautics, the predecessor of the National Aeronautics and Space Administration (NASA). He died of a heart attack in Dayton on January 30, 1948. He was seventy-six years old.

Wilbur and Orville Wright never stopped experimenting with adding innovations to their planes. Here they are seen examining a canoe attachment to one of their aircraft before its first flight over water.

FOR READING, SURFING, AND VISITING

SELECTED BOOKS

Blériot, Louis. *Bleriot: Flight into the XXth Century.* New York: Austin Macauley, 2016.

Boyne, Walter J. *The Smithsonian Book of Flight.* Washington, DC: Smithsonian Books, 1987.

Curtiss, Glenn H. and Augustus Post. *The Curtiss Aviation Book.* New York: Frederick A. Stokes Company, 1912.

Dick, Ron, and Dan Patterson. *Aviation Century: The Early Years.* Erin, Ontario: Boston Mills Press, 2003.

Grant, R. G. *Flight: 100 Years of Aviation.* New York: Dorling Kindersley, 2009.

Halpern, John. *Early Birds: An Informal Account of the Beginnings of Aviation.* New York: E. P. Dutton, 1981.

Josephy, Alvin M., ed. *The American Heritage History of Flight.* New York: Simon & Schuster, 1962.

Lieberg, Owen S. *The First Air Race.* New York: Doubleday and Company, 1974.

Mackworth-Praed, Ben. *Aviation: The Pioneer Years.* London: Studio Editions, 1990.

McCullough, David. *The Wright Brothers.* New York: Simon & Schuster, 2015.

Nevin, David. *The Pathfinders.* Alexandria, Virginia: Time-Life Books, 1980.

Prendergast, Curtis. *The First Aviators.* Alexandria, Virginia: Time-Life Books, 1980.

Roseberry, C. *Glenn Curtiss: Pioneer of Flight.* Syracuse, New York: Syracuse University Press, 1991.

Thomas, Lowell, and Lowell Thomas Jr. *Famous First Flights That Changed History.* New York: Doubleday, 1968.

Villard, Henry. *Contact! The Story of the Early Aviators.* New York: Dover 2002.

Wohl, Robert. *A Passion for Wings: Aviation and the Western Imagination, 1908–1918.* New Haven: Yale University Press, 1994.

SELECTED WEBSITES

AVIATION PIONEERS
https://www.nps.gov/articles/aviation-pioneers.htm

A DARING FLIGHT/A SOARING OBSESSION.
FLYING ACROSS THE ENGLISH CHANNEL
https://www.pbs.org/wgbh/nova/bleriot/louis.html

DISCIPLES OF FLIGHT, FIRST FLIGHT: THE EARLY AVIATORS
https://disciplesofflight.com/first-flight-early-aviators

THE FIRST AIR RACES
http://www.thefirstairraces.net/meetings/re0908/events.php

THE FIRST SUPER SPEEDWAY, RHEIMS AIR SHOW 1909
https://www.firstsuperspeedway.com/articles/rheims-air-show-1909

GRACE'S GUIDE TO BRITISH INDUSTRIAL HISTORY, HENRY FARMAN
https://www.gracesguide.co.uk/Henry_Farman

GRACE'S GUIDE TO BRITISH INDUSTRIAL HISTORY, LOUIS PAULHAN
https://www.gracesguide.co.uk/Louis_Paulhan

HUBERT LATHAM: FRENCH AVIATION PIONEER
https://peoplepill.com/people/hubert-latham-1/

THE LIFE AND TIMES OF GLENN HAMMOND CURTISS
http://aviation-history.com/early/curtiss.htm

RHEIMS: THE FIRST INTERNATIONAL AVIATION MEETING
http://www.thosemagnificentmen.co.uk/rheims

WONDERS OF WORLD AVIATION, THE FIRST AIR MEETING AT RHEIMS
https://www.wondersofworldaviation.com/rheims.html

PLACES TO VISIT

GLENN H. CURTISS MUSEUM

    8419 State Route 54

    Hammondsport, NY 14840

    607-569-2160

    https://glennhcurtissmuseum.org

Contains a vast collection relating to early aviation and to the accomplishments of Glenn H. Curtiss, including his career as a champion bicyclist, motorcycle racer, leading pioneer aircraft builder, and record-breaking pilot.

INTREPID SEA, AIR & SPACE MUSEUM

    Pier 86

    12th Avenue and 46th Street

    New York, New York 10036

    212-245-0072

    https://www.intrepidmuseum.org/

Located on the aircraft carrier USS *Intrepid*, the museum features thirty aircraft, including several recently in service. The museum also houses interactive exhibits, such as a virtual flight zone.

THE MUSEUM OF FLIGHT

    9404 East Marginal Way South

    Seattle, Washington 98108

    206-764-5700

    https://www.museumofflight.org/

Contains more than 150 aircraft, from examples of the earliest planes to airplanes on the cutting edge of modern aviation. Also on-site is the Air Force One plane that carried presidents Eisenhower, Kennedy, Johnson, and Nixon.

NATIONAL AIR AND SPACE MUSEUM

 Independence Ave at 6th St. SW

 Washington, DC 20560

 202-633-2214

 https://airandspace.si.edu/visit/museum-dc

Houses the largest collection of historic air and spacecraft in the world, from the original Wright 1903 Flyer to the Apollo 11 module.

NATIONAL NAVAL AVIATION MUSEUM

 1878 S. Blue Angel Parkway

 Pensacola, Florida 32508

 850-452-3604

 https://www.navalaviationmuseum.org/

Houses thousands of aviation artifacts and 150 navy, Marine Corps, and Coast Guard aircraft. Allows visitors to "take a ride" in the museum's flight simulators.

WRIGHT BROTHERS NATIONAL MEMORIAL

 1000 North Croatan Highway

 Kill Devil Hills, NC 27948

 252-473-2111

 https://www.nps.gov/wrbr/index.htm

This national park features the locations where the Wright brothers tested their first aircraft. A museum on the site houses a collection of the models the brothers built and the machinery and tools they used on the way to their historic achievement.

SOURCES

**THE FOLLOWING SOURCES HAVE BEEN
PARTICULARLY IMPORTANT IN PRESENTING
KEY CONCEPTS IN THIS BOOK:**

+ *A Passion for Wings* by Robert Wohl is most useful, particularly for the book's insights into Wilbur Wright's 1908 and 1909 flights in Europe, the race to be the first to fly across the English Channel, and the Grande Semaine d'Aviation de la Champagne.

+ Owen S. Lieberg's *The First Air Race* is most helpful in providing detailed accounts of Rheims air meet's physical setup and its world's fair–like atmosphere as well as for the descriptions of the event's pilots and their planes.

+ David McCullough's *The Wright Brothers* is undoubtedly the best book written about the life and accomplishments of Orville and Wilbur Wright. It also provides valuable insights into the various pioneer aviators, including Henry Farman, Louis Blériot, and Glenn Curtiss.

+ The *Curtiss Aviation Book* by Glenn Hammond Curtiss provides a detailed personal account of the aviator's life and career. In particular, it features Curtiss's own account of his Gordon Bennett Cup–winning flight at Rheims, his description of the start of his airplane-manufacturing company, and his predictions about the future of aviation.

+ Rheims: The First International Aviation Meeting was a most helpful web page in providing an excellent day-by-day summary of the events and happenings during the week that changed the world of flight forever.

ACKNOWLEDGMENTS

I am most appreciative of the contributions that Maia Walsh, Pat Pulsifer, Susan Wilson, Michelle Cote, and Carol Sandler made to this book. Many thanks are also due to Patrick and Diane M. Collins and Donna Mark for the book's outstanding design and Chandra Wohleber and Diane Aronson for so thoroughly checking the accuracy of every statement. Most of all, I am in debt to Susan Dobinick, not only for her acknowledged editing skills but for her invaluable aid in shaping the volume and her continual enthusiasm and support.

PHOTOGRAPH CREDITS

Courtesy of Mirrorpix/Getty Images: pages i, 94, 112, 122; ullstein bild/Getty Images: v, 48, 88; Library of Congress: vi, 2, 24 (right), 26, 54, 55 (top), 55 (bottom), 62, 63, 81, 92, 109, 116, 121, 130, 141, 151, 152, 158, 159, 166, 169, 172, 174, 186; Smithsonian Air and Space Museum: 4, 11, 14, 22, 24 (left), 32, 35, 40, 45 (top), 57, 58, 64 (bottom), 66, 73, 76, 87, 90, 102, 111, 118, 128, 132, 145, 164; *Süddeutsche Zeitung* Photo/Alamy Stock Photo: 7; Science & Society Picture Library/Getty Images: 18, 28; Wikimedia Commons: 30, 38, 39, 47, 82, 97, 161 (top), 161 (bottom), 163, 165, 168 (top), 168 (bottom), 170, 173; Hulton Archive/Getty Images: 36, 75, 104, 154; Trinity Mirror/Mirrorpix/Alamy Stock Photo: 42; De Agostini/Getty Images: 44; Popperfoto/Getty Images: 49, 50, 69, 78, 80, 113, 160, 167 (top); Illustrated London News Ltd/Mary Evans: 51; Aviation History Collection/Alamy Stock Photo: 52; author's collection: 64 (top); ullstein bild/Granger: 68; GL Archive/Alamy Stock Photo: 70; Historic Images/Alamy Stock Photo: 85; Lordprice Collection/Alamy Stock Photo: 99; Chronicle/Alamy Stock Photo: 100; Corbis/Getty Images: 101; Wright-Brothers.org: 110; Archive Photos/Getty Images: 114; Michael Ochs Archives/Getty Images: 135; Alpha Stock/Alamy Stock Photo: 138; The Print Collection/Getty Images: 167 (bottom); Universal Images Group North America LLC/Alamy Stock Photo: 171.

INDEX

Wright, Wilbur, *1, 173, 174*
    absent from Rheims air meet, 34,
      60
    accident of, 10–11
    biography of, 172–174
    clothes of, 9
    craftsmanship of, 6
    doubters of, 8
    in Europe, 5–16
    fans of, 11–12
    fifty-seven second flight of, 1–2
    first flight in France, 7–10
    flight demonstrations in France, *7,*
      10–13, *11*
    flight lessons given by, 12–13
    passengers of, *11,* 12
    patents secured by, 3, 4
    plane repaired by, 5–7
    plans of, 2–3
    popularity of, 11–12, 15
    pre-flight routine of, 9
    public skepticism about flight of,
      3–4
    records set by, 13, 78
    Tissandier (Paul) taught by, 45
    tricks performed by, 9, 10
    work ethic of, 6–7
Wright Company, 174
Wright Flyer. *See* Flyer
Wristwatch, 96–97, *97*

Zeppelin, Ferdinand von, 120
Zodiac (airship), 124